COMBOS

FOR YOUTH GROUPS

VOL. 3

6 MONTH-LONG THEMES WITH THE WORKS

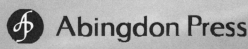 Abingdon Press

MANUFACTURED IN THE UNITED STATES OF AMERICA

Marcey Balcomb, author of *Single-Digit Youth Groups: Working With Fewer Than 10 Teens* (Abingdon Press), puts her experience to work in "Color My World." Marcey is the youth director for Common Cup Youth Ministries, a cooperative youth ministry of five churches in Portland, Oregon.

Sherri Baierl is a first-time writer with a passion for Christ and for youth. You might say she's "Fired Up!" Her day-to-day work is with Life Promotions, a ministry instilling hope in youth. She is a member of Green Bay Community Church in Green Bay, Wisconsin.

Jason Schultz, author of *Marking Milestones and Making Memories: Looking Back, Looking Forward* (Abingdon Press), focuses on relationships in "It Takes Two . . . or More!" Jason is the youth director at Edmonds United Methodist Church in Edmonds, Washington.

Barb McCreight adds "Under Construction" to her list of other *Combos* she has written. She loves building up the youth at First United Methodist Church in Bryant, Arkansas, where she serves as youth director.

Walt Marcum, author of *Claim the Name: Confirmation Teaching Plans for 39 Weeks*, gives us "Good Book Look," a short course on the Bible—its history, content, and importance for us today. Walt is pastor to youth and families at Highland Park United Methodist Church in Dallas, Texas.

Mark Youngman, a frequent writer for *Bible Lessons for Youth*, is associate pastor at First United Methodist Church in Tullahoma, Tennessee. Mark's contribution to this *Combos* is "House of Faith."

05 06 07 08 09 10 11 12 13 14—10 9 8 7 6 5 4 3 2 1

 # contents

CReate YouR

Basic Menu

Games
Build relationships as you have fun!

Share and Care Groups
Care for one another; experience a loving community; start to think about the topic.

Focus Point
Use a visual or dramatic way to start the thinking.

Focus Thoughts
Connect the Christian faith to the lives of your youth.

Focus Group
Give students a way to process what they've heard and done.

Closing
Provide reflection and commitment time.

Fixin's

Munchies
Serve food with a message!

Popular Music
Capture the attention of the youth.

Worship & Praise Music
Make God Smile!

Other Movie Options
Use these instead of the recommended video for Focus Point, if you choose.

Create-a-Video Ideas
Put your students to work on the theme!

On-the-Street Interviews
Get opinions from others to jump start the group.

Instead of a Message
Try a book or a panel.

Out and About Ideas
Go off-site for insight!

Service Project Ideas
Put faith into action.

Announcement Ideas
Add zest to the rest.

Special
Add an unforgettable event or service.

More Closing Ideas
Choose from suggested rituals, readings, and remembrances to remind your youth of God's love for them!

Leader Helps

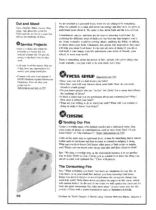

Leader Scripture Exploration
Learn from additional Bible passages related to the theme.

Talk Tips
Add a touch to make the talk livelier and more engaging.

OWN COMBO

PUBLiCitY & DeCORatiOns

Appetizers

Choose from these great ideas to publicize the theme—not only to your group members but also to their friends and the community. You're inviting youth to come to Christ!

Spice It Up!

Create an inviting atmosphere. Crank up the fun! Let the walls and the space shout your message!

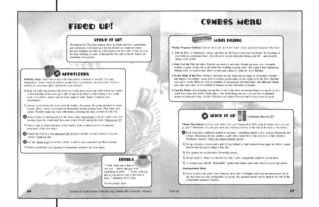

CD-ROM StUFF

Recipes

Create food that is good, fun, and says something about the theme.

Additional Games

Choose a different game if none of the others suit you.

Additional Questions

Take the conversation in a different direction if that's what your group needs.

Handouts

Give students the tools they need.

How-to Instructions

Provides the information needed to make a burning bush or do a witness statement, for example.

Focus Thoughts

Start with the text of the printed version to prepare your own talk for your own youth. Add your personal stories; put the message in the context of your youth group and community.

Theme Logos

Use the art to build your publicity flyers, t-shirts, and decorations.

On Screen Presentations

Go high-tech and big screen! Reinforce your words with powerful images.

Posters

Send home or hang up cool posters.

Scripts

Print out the scripts to the skits so your youth can easily present them.

Youth Witness Statements

Read these for inspiration and for an example of a witness statement.

Worship Helps

Use these ready-to-go worship ideas, guided meditations, litanies, and other helps.

Fired Up!

Tend the Fire of Your Soul

That is an Offering YOU Make to God

THEMES—
LESS WORK! MORE IMPACT!

COMBOS *is theme-based programming. Why use themes? There are benefits for you and your group!*

Themes help you be prepared each week. Creating a weekly program can be a daunting task even for the most accomplished of speakers and program developers. When you use a theme, such as "Rescue 9-1-1," you create a road map to guide your thinking and increase your impact. You can begin putting together songs, games, video clips, food, needed volunteers, and publicity weeks in advance. You can even assign jobs to key volunteers and youth leaders.

Themes also keep you from focusing on the same topics over and over (which gives youth permission to drop out).

Themes provide week-to-week connection but do not require week-to-week attendance for youth in two-house families.

Themes make it easier to advertise. Publicity helps parents know what is going on. It also helps students know when to invite their friends and when topics might not be appropriate for their friend's first visit.

Themes help you develop ideas that will appeal to your current youth participants and help your church reach out to new youth.

Themes allow youth to have fun while, at the same time, exploring serious life and faith issues. The programs deal with topics relevant to youth, such as dating, being authentic, placing God first, making and keeping friends, and persevering through hard times. The programs focus on being a Christian, making decisions as a Christian, and discovering God's purposes for life. The messages, small group time, discussion, worship, and service projects are specifically designed to help students grow in their faith.

Themes generate more creativity. Since you know what programs are coming up, you will be more apt to think about things that relate to the topic—and have time to pull them off. Feel free to add ideas of your own. These programs are guidelines for your use. Omit or change anything that doesn't fit your particular setting. Use every tool at your disposal to spread the Word.

YES, BUT WE DON'T HAVE ...

The Numbers

If you have fewer than ten teens, COMBOS might not be for you. Instead, check out *Single-Digit Youth Groups: Working With Fewer Than 10 Teens* (Abingdon Press). However, you don't have to have a hundred or even twenty youth to put together a dynamic Combo! Share and Care or Focus Groups can be as few as three or four. Instead of six teams for a game, two teams are just fine. You don't have to do a stand-up "talk"; sit down together and do a discussion around the points you would have made. COMBOS is highly adaptable.

The Space

Does the image of a full-sized gymnasium cast a pall on your enthusiasm? That size room is not essential; you may need to be creative with the space you have, but you can fix a Combo that will fit. Consider using the sanctuary for the Focus Point, Focus Thoughts, Focus Group, and Closing. Share and Care Groups can meet in corners of larger rooms or in multiple smaller rooms. Adapt games for smaller spaces, or play outside.

The Equipment

You certainly may use projection equipment, but you do not have to. Youth groups of all sizes have managed without VCRs or PowerPoint® for years. Choose other options or use printed sheets, instead of projected words. Have students look in Bibles, instead of on screen. Teach a new song by singing one line at a time and having the youth repeat the line, then singing the song several times. You can do it! (Just think, you don't have to worry about the equipment not working!)

The Adult Leaders

One thing about COMBOS is that adult volunteers don't have to feel that they must "do it all" or be "the expert." Having the pieces of the Combo identified means that you can ask *specific people*—adults and youth—for *specific help,* which is more easily given. One person can fix food; another lead games. For more on leaders, see page 9.

SHARE AND CARE GROUPS VS. FOCUS GROUPS

Both "Share and Care Groups" and "Focus Groups" are used in COMBOS. Do you need both? That's up to you. Here are descriptions of what they are intended to do. You get to put together whatever works best for you.

Share and Care Groups: Checking In

Student ministry focuses on Jesus' commandment to "love one another" as the heart of our faith. Share and Care Groups (or whatever you decide to call them) teach students how to love. Something about opening our lives to one another puts us in the presence of God. Many sharing experiences are from the most intimate moments of life—truly, a path to holy ground.

In a Share and Care Group, students are able to talk openly about what is going on in their lives—their joys and their struggles (highs and lows of the week). These groups provide safe spaces and people who really listen to and support one another. Group members become very close. They develop the *koinonia,* or fellowship, that the New Testament speaks of and students long for.

To achieve that level of intimacy, consider these guidelines:

• Have the same persons in the same group each week.
• Keep the group small (four to seven persons).
• Group by same gender.
• Stress consistent attendance; ask that students let someone in the group know if they must be absent. It takes time to develop a community of friends who trust one another and care deeply about each other.
• Work with your leaders so that they grow in their group leadership skills.

When Share and Care Groups meet, the student or adult leader for the particular group begins the time with prayer. Then each group member tells a high and a low for the past week. Or if time is limited, the leader may ask whether anyone had anything really good or bad happen during the past week. Individuals with serious issues may ask the leader for time to tell a personal concern prior to or after the meeting. Groups end the "checking-in" time with prayer requests and prayer led by a student.

An adult or a mature youth can be a group leader, responsible for the well-being of his or her group. The leader

• Reminds group members to listen carefully with their ears and hearts, focusing on the person who is speaking and being careful not to interrupt.
• Helps group members understand one another's feelings and learn to love God, others, and themselves.
• Does not allow group members to talk about persons who are not present. This is not a gossip session.
• Allocates time so that all persons have a chance to talk.
• Encourages members to pray daily for the group.

Leaders may also have activities outside of the regular meeting time, keep in touch during the week by e-mail or phone, and send birthday cards to group members.

A Share and Care Group is literally a laboratory for life. What is learned is used over and over outside the group. Learning how to heal one broken relationship helps an individual work on other relationships. Learning how to weather one crisis helps an individual face the next.

Share and Care Groups: Warm Up

Depending on the time, Share and Care Groups can also start the youth thinking about the topic. Within the safety of the group, the youth can begin talking about their perspectives and experiences related to the topic. COMBOS provides questions, but you may choose to select others from the Focus Group list, from the extra ones on the CD-ROM, or ones that you create yourself.

Focus Groups: Study and Discussion

In contrast to the Share and Care Groups, Focus Groups function more for the moment. The "group" is formed at the time; it does not have the continuity of a Share and Care Group. Focus Group time is for debriefing the message, for taking it further, for personalizing its impact. The assignment for the group may be Bible study, discussion, or a specific activity.

 Check the CD-ROM for the questions for both the Share and Care Warm Up and the Focus Group. You can customize the questions, print them, and give them to other adult or youth leaders to use to facilitate discussion.

MUSIC AND WORSHIP

COMBOS *gives you two types of music suggestions: popular songs and worship and praise music. Draw from the lists ones that appeal to you and your group; feel free to add other favorites.*

Popular Songs

Play these during welcoming, transitions, or exiting times. Having popular songs as part of the youth group experience engages youth, especially those who do not attend regularly. For some students, hearing popular songs dispels some negative preconceived notions about "church."

Worship and Praise Music

Music is important to youth—not just what they listen to on radios or their CD players. Music as an integral part of worship speaks to hearts and gives voice to faith.

Depending on your schedule, you may want to have more than one time of worship and praise music.

Consider creating a band of your own. (Information on CD)

Worship: Create Space for God to Work

Worship points people to God. It is not a feeling or formula. Focus energy on a single point and keep it simple.

Remind youth leaders that they are lead worshippers not performers (this is a challenge for many youth). Help them be prepared. ALWAYS offer encouragement. Hold your leaders accountable for personal growth and private worship.

After each worship, ask: Did God smile?

Fundraising Ideas for Service Projects

Drag Racing: Design a race track on a wall of the church gym or activity center using colored duct tape. Decide a monetary goal and place a sign with that number at the finish line of the track. At the beginning of the track place a construction paper car with the word "girls" and another one with the word "boys" on it. Sit two large plastic jugs on the floor under the track. Throughout the month have the entire congregation bring in loose change to put in one of the jugs. Move the cars along the track to symbolize the amount of money collected and which team is ahead. At the end of the month (or when the goal is reached, whichever comes first), declare the winner based on which group collected the most money. Winners then get to "pie in the face" (pie pans with whipped cream) the losing team!

Brick Paperweights: Decorate bricks using paints. Have youth write a favorite Bible verse on each one. Glue felt to the bottom so that it will not scratch the surface of a desk or table. Sell the bricks for $1 each to raise money for your next building or repair project!

Keys to the Kingdom: Contact a local hardware store for a donation of keys left over from their key-cutting machine. Using yarn or twine, attach the key to a small tag that says "Thank you for helping build up God's kingdom!" Then sell these keys for $1 each. After the project is over, invite all key holders to an appreciation dinner; give testimonies and show pictures or a video of the project.

—Barb McCreight

Leadership

Using COMBOS *gives you a great vehicle for involving various people in leadership—adults and youth. You can ask them to do discreet tasks as well as work as a leadership team—two great ways to develop leadership!*

Plan

Start with the youth. Gather your student leaders, and ask them to look over the Combos. Talk about how to customize each program. (Having the student leaders meet first will show you what really appeals to youth.)

Add your adult leaders. Have a student present the plans and then allow the total team of student leaders and adults to come up with more ideas. (Some adults may be taken aback by being left out of the initial planning session. Help them see that it is important that you hear from the youth in an uninhibited situation. Let them know that adults do play an important role. You are not shutting them out or rejecting their skills.)

Map out two to three months. Have your student and adult leaders develop a strategy to carry out the plans. Divide the team into work groups (games, worship, service, food, publicity). If a work group needs more help or expertise, they may invite/draft other adults or students for the specific task. (And when persons feel successful at one task, they are more willing to serve in other ways.)

Go for it! Advertise in every way you can. Some ideas are included in this book for you to use as a springboard. Encourage your group to come up with more ideas. Order some t-shirts. (You may want to give your leaders a complimentary t-shirt for all their hard work.) Decorate your space. And have a blast!

Lead by Example

Here is a sampling of specific tasks that adult and student leaders can perform weekly:

Before the Program Begins
• Greet students.
• Help with student sign in.
• Look for visitors and help connect them with other students.

• Help in the kitchen with food and drinks.
• Set up for games.
• Cue up anything to be projected.

During Games, Program, Worship
• Help communicate game rules and objectives.
• Spread out across the room during the program time.
• Remember to be first to clap and sing.
• Without causing a scene, encourage students to be quiet and listen.
• Help keep Focus Groups on task.

After the Main Session
• Say goodbye to as many students as possible.
• Help clean up.

Share and Care Group Leaders
• During the week, write or call students who were absent from your small group.
• Pray for your group members.

Up-Front Leadership Opportunities

Here are some ways to involve students in leadership and to develop their leadership skills:

• Making announcements—The task is to communicate, but to do so in a way that is fun and memorable.

• Giving a witness statement—See the CD-ROM for help in preparing a testimony.

• Explaining a game, leading the singing, reading Scripture, leading a closing ritual.

Behind the Scenes

All adult and student leaders are expected to commit to their own spiritual growth through regular participation in congregational worship, prayer, Bible study, and other spiritual disciplines.

Leaders who are strong in their faith and faith practices will set the tone for others and undergird the ministry as a whole.

sample schedules

COMBOS *are meant to fit your timeframe. The larger the group you have to manage, the more tightly you will want to adhere to a planned schedule. Here are some sample schedules, including a "cue sheet."*

Sample Two-Hour Block

6:00	Games and Food
6:25	Share and Care Groups
6:50	Program (Focus Point, Focus Thoughts, Focus Group)
7:50	Worship
8:00	End

Sample One-Hour Block, especially for Middle School

6:00	Food and Games
6:25	Program (Focus Point, Focus Thoughts, Focus Group—Abbreviated)
6:55	Worship
7:00	End

Sample One-and-One-Half-Hour Block

6:00	Share and Care Groups
6:25	Program (Focus Point, Focus Thoughts, Focus Group—Abbreviated)
7:10	Worship
7:20	Food and Socializing
7:30	End

Sample Program and Cue Sheet

5:30	Welcome/Sign In/Nametags
5:40	Food and Games
6:00	Countdown Video or PowerPoint®
6:05	Band Jam/Popular Song (Throw out t-shirts to get youth excited or have a drawing for a cool prize.)
6:08	Opening Celebration (2–3 fast worship songs by the band or taped with words on screen)
6:18	Welcome and announcements (guy and girl co-hosts, written in advance); make this time funny as well as informative.
6:22	Program Introduction (Speaker)/Student Prayer
6:25	Focus Point Skit, Activity, or Video Clip
6:30	Scripture/Message by Speaker
6:50	Small Groups (in the meeting room to avoid moving from room to room)
7:20	Student Participation (witness statement, solo, dance, art on PowerPoint, poem…)
7:25	Worship (2–3 slow songs, 3 fast songs)
7:50	Closing/Sending Forth
8:00	End

10 Tips for Playing Games

1. Use games to attract new teens, to help them connect with others, and to ensure they'll want to come back!

2. Be prepared. Have all the supplies ready to go.

3. Use existing groups (small groups, grade groups, gender groups) to avoid wasting time creating teams.

4. Give instructions clearly and quickly. Keep them simple. Go over activities with leaders in advance.

5. Be excited! Remind your adult and student leaders that they set the tone for others to follow.

6. Remind adults they are to play too. They are not the group police. They are relationship builders.

7. As the leader, look for chances to play! This allows students to see a different side of you.

8. Avoid games that waste food. (People are hungry.)

9. Never force a student to play. Allow for spectators.

10. If a game goes bad (and they do!), laugh and simply enjoy your group members.

THE Talk

COMBOS gives you a section called Focus Thoughts. Although occasionally this time may vary in format, for the most part these are talks, or the "message." Whether or not you use the talk, be sure to read it because it ties together all the pieces of the theme.

Master Teacher

Focus Thoughts is your opportunity to share yourself, your thoughts, your dreams, your vision, and God's word. You can become the master teacher for your group. Don't be shy! Try it!

On the CD-ROM is the text or outline of the printed message. Use it as a beginning point for developing your own talk. Work with the text to customize it. To be effective in this medium, you really need to adapt the content to fit who you are and who your students are. Add personal stories of your own and references to your own group's experiences that will make it come alive for your particular youth.

Be sure that you, as a youth leader, have earned the right to be heard before you try to take your group into deep waters, dealing with touchy teen subjects. If your youth know that you care about them, you can say some things in a very direct way.

Talk Tips

Do a Scripture search and study of your own when preparing your particular talk, even if you use what is given here as the base. Start with the Focus Scripture, then expand to the Leader Exploration Scriptures given in the margin. Decide what will be the heart of your message. God may lead you in a different direction, more toward what your students need.

Tell personal stories. These make you more real and approachable, as well as give students concrete examples of what you mean.

Have the students talk about a question you ask. You can do this within the talk, "Nudge your neighbor" is an easy way to engage students with one another as well as with the topic. You may also ask students to "fill in the blank" verbally as you leave open some element and ask them to supply the information. Try asking them to repeat something you have just said. These techniques make the talk more interactive and less like a sermon.

Read the Bible. If you have projection equipment, you may want to read the Scripture passage from the screen, which makes it appear as though you are part of the audience. Or read from your Bible and have students read along with what is projected. Another way to do the Scripture readings is to have student volunteers read. Be sure that they can be heard. (You may want to do some coaching on reading well in public.) Explain the passage in your own words. What is the main point (not three—just one). Never assume knowledge, especially Bible knowledge!

Write down your outline and use it when you speak. Your students will appreciate that you spent some time working on your talk—not just flying by the seat of your pants.

Have a time of reflection, and ask the group to close their eyes and think about a question you ask. Come up with a challenge for the week. Give instructions for small group discussions.

Use a video camera to record yourself so that you can learn how to improve your verbal and non-verbal communication skills.

Print each week's message in a brochure. Yes, a brochure! Giving out a printed copy will allow students and adults a chance to read what you have already said (good reinforcement!). They can also take the brochure and share it with their friends and family. Your message will become seeds for so many who might never come to hear you speak.

COLOR MY WORLD

Living in Full Color!

God calls us to live in full color. By the pictures we paint with our lives, the values we live by, the courage to live our faith out loud, and the willingness to stand for what's right and good and true, we join God in coloring our world beautiful.

APPETIZERS (Resources on CD)

Publicity Ideas: *As Christians, we are called to be "fishers of people." Simply getting a non-believing youth into the church is a huge step. Don't neglect advertising (within your church and elsewhere). God works in miraculous ways—sometimes through very small and inexpensive things. Select any or all of the ideas below. Combine or simplify. Use your imagination. Invite a team of youth to decide how to personalize each program. Create a timeline for maximum effect. Spread the word with passion.*

- Print out copies of the black-and-white coloring-book style poster. Have crayons and markers available so that youth can take turns coloring the posters the week before this unit begins. Display or distribute the posters in various places to encourage attendance, or put them all together to show the variety of ways people create—even within the lines!

- Hand out flyers cut into a simple fish shape to advertise this unit. Add dates and times. Encourage active youth to give them to friends who are not coming to church.

- Photocopy a portion of an official-looking document (Design on CD), such as the U.S. Constitution or Declaration of Independence and write your promotional information right over the top of it so that the copied document serves only as the background. Be mindful of any copyright concerns and copy only a chunk out of the middle or a vertical slice from the side—just enough to make the point.

- Make a costume to look like a crayon with arms and legs and recruit a youth to wear it for a youth group promotional spot one week ahead. Name it something like Mr. Doodle or Miss Kray-onnie. If the youth is willing to wear it around the church during coffee time or some other gathering time, you could pin a sheet of paper to the costume, with the theme and dates of your next program. Other church members will get a kick out of it.

- Find ways to use the theme logo. For example, have some T-shirts printed. Give them away as prizes.

- Wear a sign board with the information on it when making the announcements about upcoming programs and activities.

DRINKS

" 'Lord, when was it that we saw you . . . thirsty and gave you something to drink? . . .' 'Truly, I tell you, just as you did it to one of the least of these' " (Matthew 25:37, 40a).

Service project ideas

COMBO MENU

Main Dishes

Weekly Program Options: *Choose one or all; do in any order. Check each description for variations and the fixin's.*

1. **Painting Your World: Spiritual Graffiti**—We can preserve and add to the beauty of our world or to the clutter and mess. Our lives can be colorful, interesting, meaningful, helpful when we make choices to improve ourselves and our surroundings. What pictures are we painting with our lives?

2. **Following the Fish**—Just as early Christians showed others the way to the secret worship places by drawing the sign of the fish in the sand or soil, we show others the way by setting a good example with our daily lives. We can have a positive influence on those around us.

3. **Claiming and Naming**—When we claim to be Christian, we shouldn't be ashamed to let our faith show through actions and words. Do others see God through you?

4. **I Declare . . . : Making a Statement**—What do you stand for? What is God's message for us and the world? What message do *you* give by the way your choose to color your life?

SPICE IT UP (Additional ideas on CD)

Theme Decorations: *Look at your space. Use your imagination. Why settle for plain when you can go spicy? ("I'll take a taco over skinless chicken any day!") You can give away decorations as prizes at the end of the week or the theme.*

- For "Painting Your World," use a canvas drop cloth or rolls of wide paper (hung on wall if possible) to make into a graffiti wall or doodle wall. Keep it up during the whole theme and invite additions. (Be sure that whatever media you choose for the wall that it doesn't bleed through onto the actual wall.)

- For "Following the Fish," make a giant Ichthus fish symbol. Add a fishing boat, pole, or net. (Fish pattern on CD)

- For "Claiming & Naming," The Mystery Art Project becomes a picture of Jesus that can become an artistic decoration for the rest of the time.

- For "I Declare . . . : Making a Statement," make a life-size cardboard cutout of a person holding one arm up with one finger pointed (like he or she is making a point in a speech). Or make a collage from copies of famous documents or speeches, such as the Declaration of Independence, the Gettysburg Address, Martin Luther King, Jr.'s "I Have a Dream" speech, or John F. Kennedy's "Ask not . . ." speech.

PAINTING YOUR WORLD

Have It Your Way!

Choose from, adapt, or rearrange these elements to create the best soul feast for your youth group.

The Fixin's

More fun stuff to make the theme extra special! Your choice.

🔘 Munchies

- Big spiral-type lollipops with many colors
- M&M®s in lots of colors
- No-Fail Sugar Cookies in symbolic shapes (heart, star, fish, cross, person, flower, and so forth), maybe with frosting and rainbow sprinkles on top!

Popular Songs

Use these before and/or after the program to engage the youth. These are some options. Try to include the latest appropriate popular songs.

- "True Colors," by Cyndi Lauper (*The Essential Cyndi Lauper*)
- "Colour of My World," by Chicago (*The Very Best of Chicago: Only the Beginning*)
- "Ebony and Ivory," by Stevie Wonder, with Paul McCartney (*Stevie Wonder: The Definitive Collection*)
- "Yellow Rose of Texas," by The Sun Harbor Men's Chorus (*Songs of the Marines*)
- "Purple People Eater," by Kidz Jamz (*Kidz Jamz: Strawberry Jamz*)

Worship and Praise Music

- "We Are a Rainbow," by Gene Cotton (*Songs for the Journey*)
- "God of the Sparrow, God of the Whale"
- "Mountains Are All Aglow"
- "God of Wonders"

SOUL FOOD: We can preserve and add to the beauty of our world by the picture we are painting with our lives, both outwardly and inwardly. God calls us to love and care for one another and our world.

SCRIPTURE: 2 Corinthians 5:17-21 (A New Life)

🔘 GAMES (Additional game on CD)

🔘 Various Versions of Tag (Versions on CD)

Since graffiti is also called "tagging," these games are a fun play on words.

Tag Relay

Create small teams that fit your group size best. Try dividing people by the colors of their shirts, shoes, eyes, favorite colors, or anything related to colors of your choice. Be creative.

Place a large sheet of paper on the wall or on an easel in front of each team, and give each team a broad-tip marker. Provide a different color marker for each team if possible.

Have each team line up facing the paper, one behind another, with the front person at least 8–10 feet from the paper, if the room allows. At a signal, the first person in each team runs forward, grabs the marker, and writes a description of one kind of "tag" on the team's paper. He or she runs back to the team and tags (touches) the next person in line, That person repeats the process.

Here are some samples of what they might come up with: *name tag, price tag, sale tag, gift tag, size tag, coat check tag, license plate tag, red tag sale, dog tags* (combat ID), *ID tag, brand name tag, care instructions tag.* Be generous in accepting anything close to these types of answers. Award a point for each tag that is not duplicated by any other team.

🔘 SHARE AND CARE GROUPS

Checking in: Highs and lows of the week, prayer requests, and prayer

🔘 **Warm up:** Do you remembering playing Tag with your friends? Have you ever written or carved your name on a school desk, bathroom wall, bunk bed at camp, back of a bus seat? Why? What can be good about graffiti? What can be bad about graffiti? If you could influence graffiti artists to use their talents in a more acceptable way, what might you suggest as good alternatives to graffiti? (Questions on CD)

 **FOCUS POINT**

Book Option: *Old Turtle and the Broken Truth,* (by Douglas Wood and Jon J. Muth; Scholastic Press, 2003; ISBN: 0439321093). This parable is about love, acceptance, and the nature of truth. Be sure to show the beautiful watercolor illustrations. Gather the youth in a cozy and comfortable setting for reading. Then invite discussion of the story.

 Art Options: Set up your area with various art stations and supplies. Invite the youth to pick a spot and simply be creative. If they need supplies from another station, allow them to move about. At the end of the designated time, have the participants put their creations on display. Give everyone an opportunity to walk around and enjoy the gallery. Gather supplies such as crayons, markers, paints, watercolors, paper of various sizes and types, tissue paper, glue, buttons, ribbon, clay, brushes, fingerpaints, pens, charcoals, pencils, stencils, stickers, and so forth. Have water, old shirts for smocks, paper towels, and other supplies for clean-up.
(Additional art activities on CD) (Recipes for art projects on CD)

FOCUS THOUGHTS (Text on CD)

God is the Master Painter, coloring our world. Look around at the beauty of God's creation, with its infinite variety and amazing color palette.

Graffiti painters color their world too—but sometimes in ways that are inappropriate, unpleasant, and intrusive. Although some of these painters show great skill and talent, most graffiti can be just plain vandalism and a disregard for others and their property—not art. Graffiti painters are choosing how they will color their world. We have to make a choice too.

Marking places with graffiti is called "tagging." Tagging is usually related to being in a gang. People who become a part of a gang are often looking for a sense of belonging, not unlike what you can find in our youth group or in a sports team or other club. We know that gang behaviors can lead to some serious dangers. However, some of those actions raise questions for us to think about too.

Members of gangs and other groups too (us included) often wear a logo or similar clothing and use special language and symbols to show commitment to the group. But we as members can easily get caught up in destructive behavior. On one hand, the defining look and talk help us feel "in." We belong! On the other hand, conforming to others' ways of dressing and behaving can lead to loving only those who look and act like us—and to disvaluing those who do not. They don't belong! We know that God calls us to love all people and to seek justice for all, but we can lose sight of that in our need to belong. We have to make choices about how we will color our world.

Photographers who develop their own film sometimes refer to "color balance." I think God can lead us to discover how to color-balance our lives to the optimum. Life, by its very nature, means not everything goes perfectly or smoothly. But when we make choices to make our world a better place, a more beautiful place, we are painting creation right along with God.

Let's listen to today's Scripture: (*Read aloud 2 Corinthians 5:17-19.*)

The Master Painter is continuing to work, creating us into something new and wonderful. And that Master Painter is inviting us to create too,

Leader Exploration Scripture

• **Genesis 9:8-17** (God speaks with Noah about setting the rainbow as a sign of the covenant.)
• **Exodus 31:1-11** (People used their gifts to adorn the tabernacle.)
• **Proverbs 23:16** (My soul will rejoice when your lips speak what is right.)
• **1 Peter 4:10** (Use your God-given gifts to serve others.)

 ## On Screen

Key points from Focus Thoughts (PowerPoint® and Text on CD)

Out and About

Arrange transportation for the whole group and tour an area of town where there is graffiti—both destructive (like on doors or street signs) and graffiti which is more like actual art on the side of an old abandoned building or a similar setting. Discuss what you saw and discovered. What was good about it? What was bad about it?

Instead of a Message

(Learning activities on CD)

• Mystery Art Project
• Color Association
• Stereotypes on Foreheads

Service Projects

• Clean up graffiti. Check with businesses whose property has been vandalized with graffiti; offer to assist them by painting over the graffiti. They may have leftover paint stored from when the building was last painted. If not, you should be able to take a small scraping of the original paint to a paint store to match. The paint store may be willing to donate the paint for this worthy cause. Some Police Bureaus have a department or team assigned to graffiti issues and may be willing to work with you to either join their clean-up process or work from their list of places that have been vandalized. Determine who will provide paint brushes or rollers, pans, drop cloths so that you have what's needed when your group arrives to work.

• Paint a room. Choose a room in the church that could use a fresh coat of paint. Get the appropriate input and permissions, then color that space beautiful!

• Paint a Bible scene mural. In the hallway in the children's area, have someone artistic pencil in a scene from a favorite Bible story. Then work together to do the painting.

 Posters (Designs on CD)

How will you color your world?
(Doves and World)
(Coloring Book Look)

 Jesus Painter

One of the most dramatic uses of color I have seen is watching The Jesus Painter, Mike Lewis, perform Jesus Paintings, normally during a musical presentation. Right before your eyes, he transforms a large blank canvas, in a matter of minutes, into a dramatic portrait of the face of Jesus. (Contact information on CD)

"entrusting the message of reconciliation to us." God is inviting us to color our world with harmony, joy, love, justice, peace—with bringing people together—a ministry of reconciliation.

We choose to color our world in God's style by . . .

> • Caring about people and creation
> • Sharing what we have with those in need
> • Being examples of God's love
> • Serving as God's hands and feet in our place and time
> • Working for justice

So, will you choose to be part of the beauty of God's creation? Will that beauty shine through your daily life? Will you make a mark on this world that contributes to making things new? Each of us makes a choice by deciding "yes," or "no." Anything short of "yes" leaves you and world around you colorless, missing some of the most amazing experiences imaginable. What will your answer be? Let's pray.

 FOCUS GROUP (Questions on CD)

• Would life be easier or harder if you were given an instruction sheet showing you how to "paint by number"? Why, or why not?
• Would everyone's picture of life look the same as the others?
• You've heard the saying, "A picture is worth a thousand words." What does this mean to you?
• How do we begin to paint a better world?
• If your life came with a care instructions tag, just like your clothes do, what would you want yours to say?

 CLOSING

Bookmark Tag

Use the Bookmark Tag to make bookmarks. Write a prayer on the tags, then hand them out to the youth. Invite one of the youth to read the prayer aloud for the group. Then suggest to the youth that they keep the bookmark tags in their Bibles. (Pattern on CD)

I Will Color My World...

Ask youth to each name some action they will do to make a positive impact upon their world.

FOLLOWING THE FISH

SOUL FOOD: As Christians, we can invite others to follow the fish by witnessing to God's love and by setting a good example with our lives.

SCRIPTURE: Acts 1:8 (Being Christ's witnesses)

 ## GAMES

Go Fish

Hand out decks of cards to groups of three to six players. Play this familiar card game for a set time. (Instructions on CD)

Simon Says

This is a game of strategy. One person is Simon; everyone else faces the leader. When Simon gives an instruction to the players, if the instruction is preceded by "Simon says," then the players must do what is instructed. If an instruction is not preceded by "Simon says," the players must not follow the instruction. Any person following an instruction in error must step out of the play area. The last person left is the winner and becomes Simon in the next game. Strategy plays a role: Speaking fast, following patterns and suddenly breaking the pattern, starting and stopping quickly, and so forth to make it more difficult for the players to follow correctly.

SHARE AND CARE GROUPS

Checking in: Highs and lows of the week, prayer requests, and prayer

Warm up: Tell the group about a time when you went fishing. Tell about a time when others wanted you to do something you weren't sure that you should be doing. (Questions on CD)

FOCUS POINT

Video Option: *The Deep Dive,* by Jack Smith (ABC News Nightline, 1999, American Broadcasting Companies, Inc.) This is a business training video about making a better shopping cart—or any product or service. It includes a section on the fish throwers at Pike's Market in Seattle. Quite interesting and can apply to other groups or organizations. (Link to product on CD)

Have It Your Way!

Choose from, adapt, or rearrange these elements to create the best soul feast for your youth group.

The Fixin's

More fun stuff to make the theme extra special! Your choice.

Munchies

Gold Fish Crackers
Asian dried tiny fish snacks
Gummy Swedish fish
Tuna fish sandwiches

Popular Songs

Use these before and/or after the program to engage the youth. These are some options. Try to include the latest appropriate popular songs.

- "I Will Follow Him" (Chariot) (*Sister Act: Music from the Original Motion Picture Soundtrack*)
- "Follow Me," by John Denver (*Country Roads Collection*)
- "Baby Shark" campfire song

Worship and Praise Music

- "They'll Know We Are Christians by Our Love"
- "I Want to Know You (In the Secret)," by SonicFlood (*Gold*)
- "Heart of Worship," by Matt Redman (*Worship Together: I Could Sing of Your Love Forever*)
- "Still the Cross," by FFH (*Still the Cross*)
- "Down by the Riverside"

 Other Movie Options

Choose among these movies, or ask the youth to recommend a more recent release. Be sure to preview your selection to avoid any content that would be objectionable in your setting. You must have a video license. (Video licensing information on CD)

• *A River Runs Through It* (1992)
• *Finding Nemo* (2003)

Leader Exploration Scripture

• **Matthew 4:18-22, 9:9** (Follow me.)
• **Matthew 8:18-22** (Jesus encounters would-be followers.)
• **Matthew 16:24** (Take up your cross and follow me.)
• **Luke 6:35** (Love your enemies, and do good, and lend....)
• **Acts 4:1-24** (Peter and John go before the council.)

On Screen

Key points from Focus Thoughts (PowerPoint® and Text on CD)

Out and About

Go Fishing. Find a place to take the group fishing. Invite church members, family, friends who have fishing equipment to loan it and even to come along to mentor the youth. Ask the youth to bring their Bibles.

Before fishing, take turns reading aloud Scriptures about Jesus and the disciples feeding thousands with loaves and fishes—Matthew 15:29-38; Mark 6:30-44; Mark 8:1-9; Luke 9:10-17; John 6:1-14.

After fishing, read aloud Mark 1:16-20; Matthew 4:18-22.

Go Fishing for People: Read Mark 1:16-20 and Matthew 4:18-22. Talk about how to fish for people. (Example on CD)

Activity Option: Walk through the church, looking for symbols of the faith. Check out the stained-glass windows, any carvings or paintings, the altar cloths, banners, and so forth. To what do the symbols refer? What do they mean? Do this activity as a team treasure hunt with clues if you like.

FoCUS THoUGHtS (Text on CD)

God knows our hearts, our intentions, our fears, our embarrassment, our dreams, our questions, our mistakes; and you know what? God still wants to be with us through it all! That's our awesome God! When we feel separated from the love of God, we are the ones who have lost our grip—not God. It is up to us to keep our hearts and minds open to what God is doing in and through our lives—and the lives of so many other people around the world.

But keeping our own lives in line isn't the whole picture. God has shown us through the life of Jesus that we are to be fishers of all people. We are God's hands and feet in bringing others closer to God. What greater gift could we possibly offer than introducing them, or re-introducing them, to God?

I sometimes wonder how many opportunities I've missed because I didn't recognize them, didn't want to take time for them, or was worrying about myself more than anyone else. I'll never know the answer to that, but I can change the future by sharing my faith with others. Helping others grow closer to God brings us closer to God too.

The early Christians, who were persecuted for their faith, showed others the way to the secret worship places by drawing the sign of the fish in the sand or soil. The fish symbol is actually derived from the Greek word *IXTHYS* (*Ichthus*), meaning "FISH." These letters stand for the first letter of each word in the phrase Jesus Christos Theou Uios Soter (Jesus Christ, Son of God, Savior).

So, how do we today express our faith in a way that others will accept, or understand, or become curious, or at least not feel offended?

One way is simply to invite someone you know to youth group or church; follow up the invitation with an offer to pick up and bring him or her. When you invite persons to church or youth group or any related activity, you are giving them an opportunity to be among a community of believers where they can more readily recognize God's presence and activity. They may not have any idea what they are stepping into; they may be a bit leery of what that experience will be about. But then, so were those fishermen that Jesus simply told to drop what they were doing and "Follow me."

What would it be like to drop the things that cause us to be self-centered, distracted, or wasting time, and instead simply follow Jesus? It seems that there isn't anything simple about that. And, yet, that's really the key: In all the things we do and say, we are to follow the FISH, letting our faith be seen through our life.

Paul wrote a letter to the church in Thessalonica (THES-uh-luh-NIGH-kuh) giving them, and us, instructions for following the fish: (*Read aloud 1 Thessalonians 5:13b-22.*)

These are ways we show our faith with our life. We show others the way by setting a good example in our daily life. We can have a positive influence on those around us.

But "wearing our faith" counts too. (Show cross necklaces, some T-shirts with faith statements, and other items of "witness wear.") When we wear our symbols of faith, what are we saying? I used to think that these things were just for others to see, but now I also think of them as a reminder to ourselves about who God wants us to be and who we are choosing to be. They remind us how our words and actions show our values to others.

Wearing the symbols of faith may also be a way of showing we belong and that we have memories of meaningful experiences, such as retreats, mission trips, youth group, and others. We talked last time about the danger of becoming exclusive, but wearing the symbols of faith can serve as an invitation to talk about our experiences and faith. This may be one of the easiest ways we have of inviting others into conversation and ultimately of inviting them to join in the experiences that help us grow in faith. Maybe inviting others doesn't have to be so complicated. Remember, Jesus simply said, "Follow me." Let's pray.

 FOCUS GROUP (Questions on CD)
- What holds you back from sharing your faith? from inviting your friends to youth group or church? from speaking out for what is right?
- Have you ever been (or seen others be) put down or picked on about your (their) faith? Have you ever put down others for their faith?
- What would it be like to drop our distractions and follow Jesus as part of our lives here and now?
- What could help you be stronger in "following the fish"?

 **CLOSING**

Fishers of People (Fish pattern on CD)

If possible, bring in an old fishing boat (row boat) or use a toy, painting, or picture instead. If it's a real boat, turn it upside down and use it as the altar. Otherwise a table will work. Add a fish net (available at most party decoration stores in various colors if you don't have a real one) as altar decor. In advance, cut out <u>fish shapes</u> of paper for participants to write on and have crayons available for everyone.

If your group is small enough, have the group form a circle around the altar. Invite each person to write on his or her paper fish the name of someone who needs to hear about Jesus and God's hope for his or her life. Then have the youth place their fish, writing side down, on the altar as a symbol of asking God to move in a significant way in the lives of those named.

Close with prayer, including those named secretly on the fish on the altar.

 **You've Been Caught** (Closing on CD)

Service Project

Create a Coloring Book for Children: (Instructions on CD)

Art Project

Witness Wear T-shirt: As a group, brainstorm ideas of symbols, words, Scriptures and phrases that best represent your group. From that brainstorm list, select the best few items. Then develop a group design to put on T-shirts. Either have the group, or a recruited individual do the actual drawing, by hand or on computer, for the shirt. Decide on colors, make a list of every person's requested shirt size, and get shirts printed for the group members. It may turn out that the design would also be of interest to others and you could sell additional shirts as a fundraiser.

Youth Witness Statement

Ask one or two students to tell about an experience of inviting someone to church or youth group. (How-to on CD)

Have It Your Way!

Choose from, adapt, or rearrange these elements to create the best soul feast for your youth group.

The Fixin's

More fun stuff to make the theme extra special! Your choice.

Munchies

- Alphabet cereal
- Foods and drinks with the names of people or characters—Cap'n Crunch®, Spider-Man™, Cereal, Mr. Pibb®, Dr. Pepper®

Popular Songs

Use these before and/or after the program to engage the youth. These are some options. Try to include the latest appropriate popular songs.

Invite the group to think up other songs with names; see if they can sing the chorus or first few lines of the song where the name is used.

- "Barbara Ann," by Beach Boys (*Good Vibrations*)
- "Hey, Jude," by the Beatles (*The Beatles 1*)
- "Mandy," by Barry Manilow (*Ultimate Manilow*)
- "Sign of the Cross," by Iron Maiden (*X Factor*)
- "Jenny From the Block," by Jennifer Lopez (*This Is Me ...Then*)
- "God's Will," by Martina McBride (*Martina*)

SOUL FOOD: Others will see God in or through us not just because we talk about our faith, but mostly because we live it. That takes practice.

SCRIPTURE: **2 John 1:4-6.** (We are to "walk the talk."); **James 1:22-25** (We are to be doers of the Word, not just hearers.)

 ## Games

Name Game: I'm Going on a Trip (Instructions on CD)

This classic game is fun in large groups, especially if the group members don't know one another well.

Claim Your Beliefs

Distribute small cards or slips of paper and pens. Ask each person to write a sentence on his or her card beginning with the words "I believe in God because ..." or "I know that God is real because ..." Specifically request that no one put his or her name on the cards. Have the youth fold the card or slip in half and place it in a container. Mix up the cards, then redistribute one card to each person. Invite the youth to take turns reading the card aloud; the group is allowed two guesses about who wrote it. If the person holding and reading the card recognizes the writing, he or she should not give away the name. If the group guesses the correct person, that person should say, "I claim my belief." If neither guess is correct, you say, "Who claims this belief?" The correct person then says, "I claim my belief."

 ## Share and Care Groups

Checking in: Highs and lows of the week, prayer requests, and prayer

Warm up: Tell what you know about the origin of your name and its meaning. What is your favorite color? Why? Tell the group about a time when you have felt God's presence or have seen God in another person. If you could describe God with a color, what color would you choose? Why?

Focus Point

Video Option: *Evelyn* (Scene 26 "Evelyn's Prayer") Set in Ireland in the 1950's, the film tells of a father's fight to regain custody of his children. The scene is in the courtroom where the child testifies and shares her prayer. A true story, the results of the case changed custody situations for many families.

Activity Option: Scripture Search—Names for God and Jesus. Have the youth create a room-size banner. This activity also relates to the Focus Group questions on page 22. (Instructions on CD)

 FOCUS THOUGHTS (Text on CD) (Handout on CD)

Hear the good news: God claims us! God invites us to walk alongside, to be in a relationship of love with God, through Jesus Christ.

Many of us—me included—name ourselves as Christians, as followers of Christ, as ones who love and claim God in return. But do others see God through us? through me? through you?

(*Read aloud 2 John 1:4-6.*)

Jesus gave us the commandment to "love one another." It's easy relatively easy to "talk the talk," but we must also "walk the talk."

(*Read aloud James 1:22-25.*)

When we claim to be Christian, we are called to let our faith show through both our words and our actions. We are to be doers of the Word. Love is to be the foundation of all we do in our everyday lives. We should be so immersed in love that it comes through naturally in our life. How do we get to that point?

Think about the things you do "naturally," things you do very well. While you may have some talent or inclination in that direction, mostly being able to do something "naturally" or well comes from practice. The same is true of faith. We begin with a decision to claim God, to follow Jesus. And then we must "walk in it." We must practice. We need to be continually learning and exploring and discussing and feeling what God is about in our lives and how we can show our love for God.

I know that practicing—even things we like—is sometimes hard. But that's when we remember why we are doing it. That's when we remember how much God loves us and how much we want to be loved. So I suggest that we each consider making a commitment to increase, or to improve the quality of, our spiritual practices, our holy habits. These may include attending worship, Bible study, Sunday school; being in Christian conversation, praying regularly (not just when we need help with something serious.) They may include singing, dancing, drama, writing, painting, drawing, and sharing the story of our faith journeys.

Think for a moment about what you are doing to grow closer to God. Could you give one more minute a day for a prayer? Could you give ten more minutes a day to read the Bible or study Scripture? Would you notice ten or eleven minutes of your day being unavailable for everything else? I doubt it. Yet we seem to find it hard to take even those few minutes for such an amazing blessing. Our whole lives depend on God, yet we are quick to forget to be thankful and to share the good news.

(*You may wish to read aloud the children's book* If Peace Is . . . *at this point. Be sure to show the pictures.*)

I encourage each of you to try something new or at least increase something you're already doing. Here are some simple, six-second steps you can take toward increasing your holy habits, your spiritual practices:

Worship and Praise Music

- "His Name Is Wonderful"
- "Thy Word," by Amy Grant (*The Collection*)
- "I Will Call Upon the Lord"
- "Come, Now Is the Time to Worship" (*Authentic Worship: Praise and Worship*)
- "Amazing Love," by Majestic Praise (*He Is Worthy*)

Leader Exploration Scripture

- **Romans 10:8b-17** (Confessing that Jesus is Lord)
- **2 Timothy 1:8-14** (Despite being in prison, Paul declares that he is not ashamed, for he knows the God he trusts.)

Children's Book

If Peace Is . . ., by Jane Baskwill and Stephanie Carter (Mondo Publishing, 2003; ISBN: 1590344480 [hardcover]; 1590343399 [paperback]). This very short and simple book explores what peace can mean to each person. Bright and beautiful modern drawings fill each page.

Out and About

Cemetery Visit: This field trip gives you a great opportunity to explore with the youth what they would want people to remember about them. (Additional help on CD)

Service Project

Part of being a Christian community means claiming and caring for one another. Here is an opportunity to reach beyond your usual circle.

Get a list of home-bound church members from the pastor and ask for recommendations of people who would enjoy a visit from some of the youth in the church.

The purposes are two-fold:

- First, to visit church members because you claim them as part of your community of believers
- Second, to show your care for them by listening to their stories (Have a few questions prepared about their history with the church and community. They will appreciate your interest in their lives and that you took time to seek them out.)

Prepare a small card to leave with each person as a reminder of your visit. Perhaps include a favorite Scripture verse on it as well.

- Say a 6-second prayer every time you get into a car.
- Say a 6-second prayer every time you see something truly beautiful.
- Say a 6-second prayer every time someone gives you a surprise smile.
- Say a 6-second prayer every time someone brings out your anger.
- Say a 6-second prayer every time someone does something nice to help you or speaks kindly to you.
- *Say a 6-second prayer every time you see someone hurting.*

(*Hand out pens and copies of the "Six-Second Commitment" card [handout on CD]; invite the youth to choose at least one practice they will commit to doing. Then have them put it in a purse, or wallet, or wherever they will see it often.*)

Don't let these be all you do. Instead, let them be new and ever-increasing steps in your faith walk. Cultivate an "attitude of gratitude" and a keener awareness of God in your life through these simple practices. We need to do more than talk about faith; we need to walk in it. Let's pray.

FOCUS GROUP (Additional questions on CD)

- What would you add to the Six Second Commitment?
- What other things do you do to cultivate an attitude of gratitude for all of God's blessings? What helps you become more aware of God in your life?
- What is your favorite name for God?
- Jesus often took authority to give people new names. If you were to be given a new name, what would you like it to be?

CLOSING

Claimed and Named (Text on CD)

Invite the group to stand in a circle. Have two thin, water-soluble markers ready. Start with two people next to each other and hand them the markers. They will each start in opposite directions to speed up the process. If you have a single-digit group you can use person and one marker, going one direction.

The person with the marker begins by marking a cross or star on the back of the next person's hand. While doing this he or she says, "God marks and claims you." The person being marked responds, "And I claim God." Then the newly marked person receives the marker, turns to the next person, and repeats the marks and statements. Be sure that the last person/people mark and claim the beginning people. When everyone is back in his or her place, have the group repeat after you these enthusiastic phrases:

LEADER: In the name of God, I am claimed! (*Group repeats the sentence.*)
LEADER: God knows me by name! (*Group repeats the sentence.*)
LEADER: What a team! (*Group repeats the sentence.*)
LEADER: Thank you, God! (*Group repeats the sentence.*)
LEADER: Amen! (*Group repeats the sentence.*)

I Expect to See God...

Sometimes we invite youth to talk about about where they have seen God in the previous week. This time go around the group and ask where they *expect* to see God. This approach will help them keep their eyes open.

I DECLARE . . . : MAKING A STATEMENT

SOUL FOOD: Our lives declare what we believe. We can choose to color our world in ways that reflect God's goodness.

SCRIPTURE: Acts 4:33 ("With great power the apostles gave their testimony to the resurrection of the Lord Jesus, and great grace was upon them all.")

GAMES

Telephone

If you have a small group, have the youth form one line. If your group is larger, have the youth form multiple lines of about 8–10 people. One person is the Starter. The Starter makes up a sentence and whispers it to the first person in line. In turn, that person whispers to the next person what he or she heard. Continue the telephone message on down the line. Invite the last person who receives it to tell the group what he or she heard. The Starter then tells the group whether what that person said is correct—or what the original message was. This may be repeated several times.

Follow the Leader

Find a space to spread out where there's room to move around freely. Line up one person behind another. The leader starts walking, hopping, skipping, waving arms, or doing some other movement. The rest of the followers do whatever the leader is doing. Have fun!

SHARE AND CARE GROUPS

Checking in: Highs and lows of the week, prayer requests, and prayer

Warm up: Tell the group about a time when you spoke up for yourself or someone else or when you helped spread a rumor by passing it on to others. If you played both games (Telephone and Follow the Leader), ask which game (words or actions) made it easier to get the information you needed?

FOCUS POINT

Video Option: *Spanglish* (DVD Scene 2, VHS 05:15–11:53). Flor, who speaks only Spanish, arrives at Deborah's house to interview for a job as housekeeper, bringing her cousin along as translator. Deborah, who speaks only English, does not communicate with the women well, speaking rapidly and nervously. Flor, on the other hand, who pays close attention to Deborah,

THE FIXIN'S

More fun stuff to make the theme extra special! Your choice.

Munchies

• Wax lips with red liquid inside

Popular Songs

Use these before and/or after the program to engage the youth. These are some options. Try to include the latest appropriate popular songs.

• "Sound of Silence," by Simon & Garfunkel (*Simon & Garfunkel's Greatest Hits*)
• "Don't Laugh at Me," by Mark Wills (*Wish You Were Here*)
• "Creed," by Rich Mullins (*Songs*)

Worship and Praise Music

• "I Could Sing of Your Love Forever," by SonicFlood (*Worship Together: I Could Sing of Your Love Forever*)
• "Shout to the North," by Delirious (*Worship Together: I Could Sing of Your Love Forever*)
• "Here I Am to Worship," by Tim Hughes (*Worship Together: I Could Sing of Your Love Forever*)
• "Shout to the Lord," by Hillsongs Australia (*Shout to the Lord: The Platinum Collection*)
• "Declaration of Dependence," by Steven Curtis Chapman (*Declaration*)

Other Movie Options

Use this movie, or ask students to recommend a more recent release. Be sure to preview your selection to avoid any content that would be objectionable in your setting. Remember you must have a video license. (Video licensing information on CD)

• *National Treasure* (2004)
• *Lost in Translation* (2003)

Leader Scripture Exploration

• **Psalm 89:1-2** (I will declare your steadfast love forever.)
• **Romans 12:9-21** (Paul lists the marks of the true Christian.)

Instead of a Message

Have the group discuss and write their own statement of belief or creed. (Sample on CD)

speaks clear Spanish, and maintains eye contact, communicates with Deborah successfully, even though she doesn't speak Deborah's language.

Skit Option: *Could You Put that in Writing?* This is a dialogue between God and a youth. Two youth can perform this skit for the other group members and follow with discussion. (Script on CD)

FOCUS THOUGHTS (Text on CD)

Mohandas Gandhi used his life to work toward freedom from exploitation and injustice and to further human equality, human dignity, and self-respect. He believed that those things are important and that it is possible to have peace on this earth if we could settle our differences with non-violence. Gandhi's impact on India and people all around the world was immense.

Mother Theresa believed so strongly that all people are God's children that she willingly ministered to society's "lowest of the low" at the lowest point of life—while they were dying.

Countless others whose names and stories we do not know have lived out what they believe and have had an important impact on others. We may never be recognized as a Gandhi or a Mother Theresa; but it would be sad to go through our entire lives never having taken a stand on anything that really mattered in our lives, families, and communities.

What you believe matters in how you live your life every day. Here are some examples of what I mean:

• If I believe that God loves all persons, then I treat all people with respect even if I don't agree with them. If I believe that God loves only the people who worship as Christians, then I can hate Muslims and Buddhists and Jews.

• If I believe that God created human beings as stewards or caretakers of creation, then I recycle. If I believe that God created human beings to have power over creation, then I can litter or spray-paint graffiti on rocks.

What do you believe? Take a few minutes individually to write five things that you believe about God or Jesus or church or being a Christian. When you finish your list, find a partner. The two of you will talk about what you have stated. You do not need to agree with the other person's statements—just talk about them. Tell each other what you think and why these statements are important to you.

(*Give the group several minutes to write and then talk. You may choose to invite volunteers to read some of their declarations to the whole group. This is not a time to judge anyone's statements. If you have any unease about what you hear from a youth, talk with him or her individually later.*)

Now, do the second half of the task: If I believe this, then I. . . . How does what you say you believe guide your actions? Take a few minutes again, individually, to write what actions would flow from what you believe. Then find a different partner to talk about how you see what you believe directing how you live.

(*Again, give the group some time to write and to talk. Invite volunteers to report to the whole group, if you wish.*)

Let's look at this issue from a different perspective. You've heard the words *hypocrisy* or *hypocrite*. You know that what some people say they believe and what they do doesn't match. Actions do indeed speak louder than words. Actions are the true measure of belief.

The disciples were hiding in fear because they believed that Jesus had been killed. But when they believed the Resurrection and received the Holy Spirit, their whole lives changed.

(*Read aloud* ***Acts 4:33.***)

What we believe affects how we will color our world. Your beliefs, your words, and your actions are painting a picture that will have an impact on others. Will it be a work of beauty? Will it be meaningful? Will it stand up for justice? How will you color your world? You have a choice. Let's pray.

 ## F☉CUS GR☉UP (Additional questions on CD)

- How hard or easy was it for you to identify five things you believe strongly about God, Jesus, the church, or living as a Christian?
- How hard or easy was it for you to see how actions flowed from those beliefs?
- How hard or easy was it for you to talk to your partner about what you believe and how that directs your life?
- Now that you have had the experience of talking to two other people in the group about what you believe, how will that help you be able to talk to someone else about your beliefs? How will your experience talking about what you believe help you be able to stand up for what you believe in a difficult situation?

 ## CL☉SING

 ### We Believe (Litany on CD)

Use the We Believe litany provided, or have the youth create their own statement or creed and then read it as the closing message.

Read aloud **Psalm 89:1-2** and sing "I Could Sing of Your Love Forever" as a benediction.

Coloring My World

Invite the youth to think about this question:

What are three things you could personally do to make the world around you a better place? to paint a prettier picture—one that declares God's love?

Have supplies available and give them time to paint or draw a representation of one or more of the things to which they will commit themselves. Have them write their name on their picture and bring it to the altar as a sign of their commitment. (If an altar is not available, post the pictures in the room as part of the closing, or hang them later as a reminder.

Read aloud **Psalm 89:1-2** and sing "I Could Sing of Your Love Forever" as a benediction.

Out and About

Prayer-a-thon. Hold a prayer-a-thon or vigil for a specific amount of time (for example, 12 hours overnight) and invite people in the congregation, family, and friends to submit prayer requests in advance. Dedicate the intercessory prayer time to those requests. Youth can be assigned, or sign-up, for specific shifts and other activities can be available on-going through the time so there is group building time for those not in prayer.

Service Projects

- Litter Patrol: The objectives of this project are three-fold:

  First, it is to do something positive to beautify the neighborhood you choose to work in (even though it means cleaning up messes others left behind).

  Second, it is important to donate your own time to the good of others; and it is something that can be done with your family or friends as well as with organized groups.

  Third, it is a public display of caring about your community and taking initiative without being asked. (Instructions on CD)

- Painted Rocks of Encouragement or Thinking of You Cards (Instructions on CD)

Fired Up!

Stoke It Up!

Throughout the Christian journey, there are highs and lows, questioning and excitement. God must have known all that we would encounter, because Scripture provides us with resources to live a life on fire, to keep the flame burning, to make it through the fire, and to fan the flames into something even greater.

 Appetizers

Publicity Ideas: *Select any or all of the ideas below. Combine or simplify. Use your imagination. Invite a team of youth to decide how to personalize each program. Create a timeline for maximum effect. Spread the word with fire.*

☺ Kick off with a big bonfire! Between two weeks and a week and a half before the bonfire or first meeting of the series put a pile of logs in the foyer or hall leading to the youth room. Use yellow, orange and red tissue paper to make flames. Unleash your imagination!

☺ About a week before the series, host the bonfire. Encourage the group members to invite friends. Have s'mores, and hand out information on the meeting times. Plan songs and games. Possibly make the event with dinner, including hot dogs cooked over the fire.

☺ At the bonfire or meeting prior to the series, make <u>matchbooks</u> to invite youth to the next meeting; have the youth hand them out to their friends during the week. (<u>Design on CD</u>)

☺ Show a tape or project pictures of the bonfire at the weekend services to increase awareness of the new series.

☺ Search the web for a free <u>animated GIF of fire</u> to include on your website or in your e-mails. (<u>Link on CD</u>).

☺ Use the (<u>theme logo</u>) for posters, flyers, T-shirts to get youth fired up about coming!

☺ Hold a candlelight vigil, praying for something related to the four topics.

Drinks

" 'Lord, when was it that we saw you . . . thirsty and gave you something to drink? . . . ' 'Truly, I tell you, just as you did it to one of the least of these' " (Matthew 25:37, 40a).

Service project ideas

COMBOS MENU

 ## Main Dishes

Weekly Program Options: *Choose one or all; do in any order. Check each description for the fixin's.*

1. **Life on Fire**—Commitment, energy, and time are the keys to knowing God better. By investing in your faith on a consistent basis, you will grow in your faith and change your life—and possibly change your world!

2. **Don't Let the Fire Go Out**—Tragedy can strike at any time, friends can leave you. Or maybe nothing is going wrong, but at the same time nothing is going right—life is just a little depressing. During trials, we need to have places to turn and a place to "plug in" as a Christian.

3. **In the Midst of the Fire**—Being a Christian can test what you are made of. Sometimes friends— and maybe even family—tease you or exclude you because you are trying to be the best Christian you can be. In the Bible are a lot of examples of persecution and misfortune; and although change may take some time, God is faithful in helping us deal with times of trouble.

4. **Fan the Flame**—Encouraging one another is one of the most overlooked things we can do to, in a small way, make this world a better place. One small thing you say or do can have a dramatic impact on someone's day—or life. God gives us a spirit of power and of love to use for good.

 ## Spice It Up (Additional ideas on CD)

Theme Decorations: *Look at your space. Use your imagination! Why settle for plain when you can go spicy? Remember, you can give away decorations as prizes at the end of the week or the theme.*

Each week pick a different method to decorate—something related to fire, such as Polynesian tiki torches, Polynesian fire pit, candles, a grill with a small fire or fake fire in it, a fake fireplace, flashlights, lanterns. (Party decoration website on CD)

Set up a fireplace screen with a pile of logs behind it. Stuff colored tissue paper in yellow, orange and red into the logs to shape a fake fire.

Fire engines are an alternative decorating theme.

On the week of "Don't Let the Fire Go Out," a fire extinguisher might be a good prop.

A warning sign with the "flammable" symbol that marks trucks may also be a good decoration.

Announcement Ideas

Every week for the series, have someone dress like a firefighter and read announcements. He or she may bring in a fire extinguisher as a prop. The announcements can be taped to the side of the extinguisher canister if needed.

LiFe on FiRe

Have It Your Way!

Choose from, adapt, or rearrange these elements to create the best soul feast for your youth group.

The Fixin's

More fun stuff to make the theme extra special! Your choice.

💿 Munchies

Let's go for something hot!

• Olé Appetillas
• Chips and Fresh Salsa Dip

Popular Songs

Use these before and/or after the program to engage the youth. These are some options. Try to include the latest appropriate popular songs.

• "This Is Your Life," by Switchfoot (*The Beautiful Letdown*)
• "Vertigo," by U2 (*How to Dismantle an Atomic Bomb*)

Worship and Praise Music

• "Come, Now Is the Time to Worship," by Brian Doerkson (*You Shine*)
• "Create in Me a Clean Heart"
• "Refiner's Fire," (*16 Great Praise & Worship Classics 5*)
• "Awesome God" by Rich Mullins (*Essential Praise & Worship*)
• "Pass It On"
• "Consuming Fire," by Third Day (*Offerings: A Worship Album*)

SOUL FOOD: Commitment, energy, and time spent in knowing God better leads to a true life on fire.

SCRIPTURE: Acts 2:1-4 (They were filled with the Holy Spirit.)

Games

Flashlight Tag

Depending on the size of the group, have several flashlights available, and choose one or more players to be "it." For every 8 to 10 players, have one "it." Identify the boundaries of the playing area. Then the game begins; any youth hit with the beam of light become "it" and are given the flashlight. Play for a designated time period. If you choose, reward players who escaped being "it."

The Listening Game

You will need a stack of papers and a blindfold. One youth will be blindfolded; one "helpful" youth (the Holy Spirit) will have the duty of talking the blindfolded youth through the room. This person may move as needed. The rest of the youth will be "unhelpful." The blindfolded youth's objective is to reach the opposite side of the room without touching any of the sheets of paper scattered at random spots on the floor. The key is listening to the "helpful" voice that guides him or her. The rest of the youth are placed around the room, not allowed to move from their place, but allowed to hold their sheet of paper out at arm's length and talk to the blindfolded youth. Success depends largely upon to whom you listen.

💿 SHARE AND CARE GROUPS

Checking in: Highs and lows of the week, prayer requests, and prayer

💿**Warm up:** How do you know when someone is really passionate about something? Give some examples of someone you would described as "on fire" for a cause.

How are a fire and a flashlight beam different? How are they alike? Brainstorm a list. How do you think a fire and a flashlight are like the Christian faith or being a Christian? Which would you prefer your faith to resemble more? Why? (Questions on CD)

Focus Point

Video Option: *Remember the Titans* (Start: 1:39; stop: 1:41) The former quarterback talks about what he will do after his accident. He has passion for life—not just for the sport he could play when he could use his legs. In real life Gary goes on to compete in sports in his wheelchair.

Skit Option: One couple is in a forest with a lantern at night and a separate couple in a different part of the forest with a small-beam flashlight. Switch back and forth between the couples' dialogue, freezing them in place.

The first couple casually walks along, arm in arm, and talks about how dark it is, how they are glad to have light, and how they didn't realize that a lantern gave off so much light.

The second couple walks along, clinging to each other, jumping at noises, and snipping at one another about who gets control of the flashlight.

Focus Thoughts (Text on CD)

All of us have experienced being "in the dark"—either literally or figuratively. It's not a comfortable place to be. We wonder what we're going to bump into or whether someone or something is out there ready to pounce. We get a taste of what life might be like if we never saw the light again.

Jesus' disciples were in the dark of doubt and fear after Jesus' ascension into heaven. They had seen that he had risen from the dead. They had experienced that joy. But now he was gone again. Did they really see him? Would the Romans come after them too? The group was huddled together in a room, waiting, hoping that the dark would lift. And then it happened!

(*Read aloud* **Acts 2:1-4.**)

Because it was a festival time in Jerusalem, people were there from all over. Imagine how they must have felt being in that crowd, hearing things in their own language at the same time others were hearing the message in their own language. The disciples, who had been so fearful, were now speaking out boldly about Jesus Christ. Those same people were suddenly "on fire." They had been touched by the Holy Spirit—just as Jesus had promised. They came "out of the dark" and carried God's message throughout the world and through time. You and I are here today because they were "on fire" for their faith.

"Life on fire" is a pretty attractive concept. In addition to images of the disciples, the phrase draws forth stories from the movies and from real life of persons, such as William Wallace, portrayed in the movie in *Braveheart*; Neo from the movie The Matrix; and the Mothers Against Drunk Driving. These real and fictional persons' passion changed their world. Their individual causes fueled their fire even through questioning and fear. Those causes were so important that they consumed their thoughts and drove their speech. Their lives were touched and changed forever, and they made a difference in their world because they were on fire.

So, what made their particular cause so important to them? Why did they choose it? Many times the reason is simply that it became personal; and in turn, they were willing to pour their energy and time into their cause. When

Other Movie Options

Choose one of these or ask the youth to recommend a more recent release. Be sure to preview the selection to avoid any content that would be objectionable in your setting. Remember that you must have a video license.
(Video licensing information on CD)

- *Runaway Bride* (1999) (The bride finally gives up her running shoes. Before, she had wanted a real relationship so much she had faked it.)
- *Mean Girls* (2004) (Scenes that contrast authentic versus fake friendships)

Leader Scripture Exploration

- **Psalm 15** (Who shall abide in God's sanctuary?)
- **Hebrews 12:18-29** (Contrast between past [Mt. Sinai] and future [Mt. Zion]; eternal reward for those who are faithful)

Guest Speakers

- Have a missionary come talk about his or her work, including getting to know the culture and the people and the importance of a passion for Christ.
- Invite a member of MADD (Mothers Against Drunk Driving) to come tell the story of how the organization began, and why she became involved. Most frequently, members have experienced a loss of a loved one, which has ignited their passion for change.
(Information on CD)

Out and About

Have a bonfire. Make s'mores. Sing songs. Talk about life on fire for Christ and life on fire for a cause that reflects the teachings of Jesus.

◉ Service Projects

• Have a cookout and donate the proceeds to a family that has suffered a house fire. Or give the money to the Red Cross for their work.

• Call your local fire station; find out if they have any opportunities for service your group could give.

• Connect with your local chapter of SADD (Students Against Destructive Decisions). Find out what your group can do.
(Information and link on CD)

we are touched at a personal level, when we are changed by something, when we commit to a cause and invest our energy and time in it, we grow to understand more about it. The same is true about faith and the love of God.

Commitment, energy, and time are the keys to knowing God better. By exploring the different areas of faith you can find one that inspires you to act. Some examples would be serving others, studying the Bible, or talking to others about your faith. Ultimately, this action, this inspiration, this cause will help you know God better. It can start all sorts of things if you allow God lead; it can change your life and maybe your circle of friends, your school, or even your world.

There is something about the power of fire—people who glow, things that exude warmth—you just want to be near them. Let's pray.

Focus Group (Questions on CD)

• Have you ever felt excited about your faith?
• How have you told your friends about your faith? How do you invite friends to youth group?
• Do you know people who are "on fire" for Christ? for a cause that reflects the teachings of Jesus?
• Is there a cause that you are passionate about and committed to? Why? How does it reflect your faith?
• What are you willing to do to tend your faith? What will you commit to doing in order to know God better?

◉ Closing

◉ Tending Our Fire

Create a worship space with lighted candles and a darkened room. Sing some songs of praise or contemplation, such as ones from Taizé ("Lord, Jesus Christ" or "Our Darkness"). (Taizé information on CD)

A life on fire must start at a personal level; it must be something that is stirred within each of our hearts and that we have to commit to helping it along. What can you do to know God better, what areas of faith excite or inspire you? Where can you invest your energy and time and draw closer to God?

Say: "We sang a worship song at the end tonight because it is yet another way to draw closer to God. I invite you to commit to at least one thing you can do to tend your spiritual fire." Close with prayer.

The Consuming Fire

Say: "What is holding you back? Are there are situations in your life, in your heart, or in your mind that distract you from knowing God more, things you need to forgive or need forgiveness for, or regrets, things you want help with? Write them down and place the papers in this chest, which will remain locked. At the end of our series we will opened the chest and let God, the great consuming fire, take them away." (*Leave some time for this activity.*) Close with a youth benediction such as **Numbers 6:24-26.**

Don't Let the Fire Go Out

SOUL FOOD: Things can go very wrong in life; but Christians have a Source, so the fire doesn't go out.

SCRIPTURE: Leviticus 6:12-13 (The fire on the altar must be kept burning; it must not go out.)

Games

Tending the Flame

Depending on the size of your group, you may wish to divide the group into smaller teams of 8–12. Give each team a balloon or large ball. Their task is to keep the ball in the air—not letting it hit the floor. Challenge the teams to "tend the flame and not let it go out." Have each team count the number of consecutive hits. They have to start over if the ball hits the floor. Play for a designated time. If you choose, reward the team with the highest number. If you are playing with only one team, be sure to reward the group for their highest count and team effort at "tending the flame."

The Heat Is On

Send someone out of the room. Have the group choose a sign (something subtle—for example, giving the thumbs up or scratching one's head) and decide where "the sign" starts. Invite the outsider to come back in. The group will then pass the sign around the room while he or she tries to figure out who has it. To pass "the sign," one person gives the sign to another member of the group; when that person makes the sign back, it has been received. When the person in the middle guesses who has the sign, the round is over. Send someone else out, and choose a new sign. Play several rounds.

Share and Care Groups

Checking in: Highs and lows of the week, prayer requests, and prayer

Warm up: Tell about an experience of really feeling down. What helped you get through it? Where do you see hopelessness and despair among your friends or classmates? How have events like those of September 11, 2001, or the 2004 Asian tsunami affected people's thoughts about life? (Questions on CD)

Have It Your Way!

Choose from, adapt, or rearrange these elements to create the best soul feast for your youth group.

The Fixin's

More fun stuff to make the theme extra special! Your choice.

Munchies

- Bean Dip
- Tortilla Roll Ups
- Fiesta Tortilla Stackers

Popular Songs

Use these before and/or after the program to engage the youth. These are some options. Try to include the latest appropriate popular songs.

- "Wind Beneath My Wings," by Bette Midler (*Greatest Hits: Experience the Divine*)
- "Light My Fire," by The Doors (*The Best of The Doors*)
- "Respect," by Aretha Franklin (*Aretha's Best*)
- "Stayin' Alive," by Bee Gees (*Greatest*)
- "My Own Prison," by Creed (*Greatest Hits*)
- "We Didn't Start the Fire," by Billy Joel (*The Essential Billy Joel*)

Worship and Praise Music

- "After the Music Fades," by Shaun Groves (*Invitation to Eavesdrop*)
- "Eagles' Wings," by The Katinas (*Lifestyle: A Worship Experience*)
- "Did you Feel the Mountains Tremble?" (*Authentic Worship: Praise & Worship*)
- "New Every Morning," by Big Daddy Weave (*Fields of Grace*)
- "Jesus, Lover of My Soul"

Leader Scripture Exploration

- **Job 2:8** (Job sat among the ashes.)
- **Isaiah 61:3** (Beauty for ashes)
- **Romans 8:18-30** (All creation longs for God's glory and redemption.)

Instead of the Message

Read aloud the children's book, *Alexander and the Terrible, Horrible, No Good, Very Bad Day,* by Judith Viorst and Ray Cruz (Atheneum, 1972; ISBN: 0689300727). Use it as a discussion starter.

On-the-Street Interviews

- How do you deal with feeling down?
- What do you do to cheer yourself up?
- What would you recommend to someone who was depressed?

On Screen

Key points in Focus Thoughts (PowerPoint® on CD)

FOCUS POINT

Video Option: *She's All That* (Start: 26:58; stop: 29:34) The main character becomes upset and exits the party she was at with the popular boy; she says that she never wanted "them" (the popular girls) to see her cry.

Be sure to preview your selection to avoid any content that would be objectionable in your setting. Remember that you must have a video license. (Video licensing information on CD)

Skit Options:

Bad Day: An idea is to portray a really bad day. (Suggestions on CD)

Treat for the Soul: (Story on CD)

FOCUS THOUGHTS (Text on CD)

Tragedy can strike at any time; we've seen that with 9-11 and the Asian tsunami. We know that people we love can become ill, or be in an accident, and even die. Life seems fragile at times. Relationships can be fragile too. Friends can leave you, even betray you. And sometimes even nothing is terribly wrong in our lives, but at the same time nothing feels right . . . life is just depressing. We know that life will bring us "down" times. How do we get through these trials?

Let's step back a bit and hear from the Scripture. We're going to a book of the Bible that may not be as familiar to you as some. It is Leviticus, named after the Levites, who were the priests who tended to the sacrifices at the Temple in Jerusalem. Before Jesus came to take away the sin of humanity, the people made burnt offerings in the Temple as a way of showing their love for God and their desire to be right with God. In Leviticus 6:8-13, God gives instructions to the priests for those burnt offerings. Listen to these two verses; they offer us an important message for our lives today.

(*Read aloud **Leviticus 6:12-13**.*) Twice God says, "The fire must not go out."

In our culture fire often symbolizes life. We have "eternal flames" lit in churches and at gravesites around the country. It means that the memory goes on, that people take time to tend to the flame to keep it going. An eternal flame has an underlying message of importance.

How many of you have had the task of lighting a fire? (Ask for a show of hands.) Just think, in the days when this passage was written there were no matches, no newspapers to use as kindling, no nifty fire wands. Lighting a fire is not always easy even with those helps, but relighting a flame after the coals are cold is even more difficult.

Let's think now about our soul's fire. When we become burdened by this life and feel depressed, suffocated, or hopeless, it is as if we are slowly snuffing out the flame that lives inside of each of us. Sometimes it may seem easier to give up; but the reality is that it is important to hold on, to keep tending the fire. It's easy to slide down further into hopelessness and despair, to let the fire go out; but as Christians we have help in keeping the fire going.

First, when you feel yourself dwelling on the negative experiences in your life, going over and over situations that make you feel bad, remind yourself:

• *You* are a beloved child of God.
• God is *with you* even when you are hurting.
• God is working for *good* in your life (**Romans 8:28**).
• *With God's help,* you will get through this.

Talk with God; open yourself to God. Allow God to help you.

Then, turn to others to help you keep your fire going. Seek out your Christian friends (including adults); lean on those you trust for guidance and encouragement.

Choose to do something uplifting instead of dwelling on what is dragging you down. With God's help and with the help of Christian friends, you will get through this.

Tend the fire of your soul. That is an offering you make to God. Let's pray.

 **FOCUS GROUP** (Additional questions on CD)

• When does life get depressing? When do you feel overwhelmed?
• Why do you think that light is important to people?
• What do candles and fire symbolize in the Scripture?
• Talk about eternal flames (for example, John F. Kennedy has an eternal flame on his grave). What is the significance of an eternal flame?
• Back when people had no matches, why would it be better to keep a fire going?
• What does tending to a flame look like? How long would it take?
• How does the idea of "tending the fire" relate to your life?

CLOSING

The Consuming Fire

Have a sealed box available where the youth can deposit slips of paper. Have them write out bad experiences or situations where they have felt self-pity, despair, deep sadness, misdirection, or confusion. Have the youth continue to put the slips of paper in the locked box. This week encourage them to let go of things they hold onto that hold them back (for example, if has someone has said that they are stupid or said something else insulting).

Away From the Flame

Use this illustration verbally or carry it out physically with a live coal. (Be sure to attend to safety needs.) A coal (or charcoal briquette) will burn continuously as long as it is surrounded by others that are also on fire. But when the coal is removed from the fire, it will burn on its own for a time and then go out. When we remove ourselves from other Christians who are on fire for Christ, our fire will soon go out. Christ has given us the church, the community of faith, to help us tend our fires. Close with prayer.

 **Out and About**

Visit a homeless shelter, women's shelter, or a similar temporary housing facility and meet some of the people who are down on their luck. When you get back to the church, talk about what the youth saw. Did they see hope, despair, were the people making an effort not to give up on life? Ask them how they felt about seeing the people and being there. No answer is a bad answer.
(Additional idea on CD)

Service Projects

• Ask the youth to do one random act of kindness this week and to tell the group about it next week.
• Have the group get together and brainstorm ways to encourage local pastors and youth pastors.

 Poster

Tend the Fire of Your Soul
(Design on CD)

In The Midst Of The Fire

Have It Your Way!
Choose from, adapt, or rearrange these elements to create the best soul feast for your youth group.

The Fixin's
More fun stuff to make the theme extra special! Your choice.

Munchies
- Mexican Grilled Zucchini Pizzas
- Spicy Hummus
- Hotsy Totsy Snack Mix

Popular Songs
Use these before and/or after the program to engage the youth. These are some options. Try to include the latest appropriate popular songs.

- "Disco Inferno," by The Trammps (*Disco Inferno*)
- "Burn," by Jo Dee Messina (*Burn*)
- "We Didn't Start the Fire," by Billy Joel (*Piano Man: The Very Best of Billy Joel*)
- "The Heat Is On," by Glenn Frey (*Classic Glenn Frey*)
- "I Turn to You," by Christina Aguilera (*Christina Aguilera*)
- "Wind Beneath My Wings," by Bette Midler (*Greatest Hits—Experience the Divine*)
- "Standing Outside the Fire," by Garth Brooks (*In Pieces*)

Worship and Praise Music
- "Consuming Fire," by Third Day (*Offerings: A Worship Album*)
- "Potter's Hands"
- "I Need You More"
- "I Can Only Imagine"
- "Change My Heart, O God"
- "God Leads Us Along"

SOUL FOOD:
Even Christians go through fiery furnaces in life; but we have the advantage of the "fourth man."

SCRIPTURE:
Daniel 3:13-28 (Shadrach, Meshach, and Abednego are in the fiery furnace.)

Games

Pipe Cleaners—With a Twist
Give everyone two pipe cleaners (or chenille stems). Have one youth face away from the rest of the youth. He or she is to make an object with the pipe cleaners. The rest of the group is not allowed to see the shape. The youth then describes the shape to the rest of the group, without mentioning any type of object—just the direction of the twists and turns and curves the object forms. When the description is finished, the youth turns to face the group. Everyone can then compare their shapes. They will likely be radically different.

Alligator Swamp
Divide the youth into teams of 6–8. Give each team 4 or 5 squares of carpet, vinyl flooring, or cardboard. Find an area where you have approximately 20 yards from end to end. Put lines of masking or duct tape on the ground to signify the start and the finish lines. Have the youth figure out how to get their entire team from one end to the other, using their squares as safety nets to walk across the alligator swamp. Whichever team crosses the swamp first wins.

Share And Care Groups

Checking in: Highs and lows of the week, prayer requests, and prayer

Warm up: If youth did "random acts of kindness" during the week, be sure to have them talk about the experience: What did you do? How did it make you feel? Would you do something like that again? Did you notice that when you do something self-less, you feel better in general? Why do you think that is? Brainstorm other random acts of kindness that the youth could do to improve someone else's day or life.

Or have the youth each think of something to do that is just nice or that would encourage a person close to them. Invite them to tell the group their ideas and tell why they would like to do that. Remind the group that no idea is a bad idea.

⊙Focus Point

Video Option: *Armageddon* (1998) (Scene 24, "Drawing Straws") Near the end of the story the boyfriend (Ben Afleck) of the daughter of the team leader (Bruce Willis) is shoved back into the corridor, and the team leader decides to stay on the meteor and will die because of that decison. The boyfriend is torn—he doesn't want to die, but he doesn't want the team leader to either. It is a no-win situation. (End with "Son, I love you.")

Artisan Option: Invite someone (youth or adult) to talk about and show the role of fire in creating pottery, china, glass, and so forth.

⊙Focus Thoughts (Outline on CD)

Being faithful to God can test what you are made of. Sometimes friends, and maybe even family, tease you or exclude you because of your beliefs and your actions and choices. Sometimes even other Christians may exclude you because of decisions you make that they don't agree with. Sometimes life just seems to be on the attack against you. Does being a Christian mean that you stand alone in the midst of the fire?

Let's look to Scripture. Do you know what "being in exile" means? (Invite student responses.) In the history of God's chosen people, a portion of them spent many years in captivity in Babylon, far from their home in Israel. The people of God had no freedom; they were expected—even forced—to do as they were told. At one point, the king, Nebuchadnezzar, built a grand golden statue and told everyone to worship it. But Shadrach, Meshach, and Abednego were committed to worshiping only the Lord God. They refused to bow down. Let's hear the rest of the story.

(*Read aloud **Daniel 3:13-28.***)

This story is one of hope, a reminder that God is with us even in the most difficult or terrifying situations. People throughout the ages have drawn strength from this story to help them get through their personal fiery furnaces—whatever they may be.

Knowing that God is faithful may not feel like enough when we are in the midst of trials. When we are going through rough times, we just want someone to talk to, a way to find relief, a place to escape to. Often, people will want to disguise or escape from these feelings so much that they complicate their lives even more by turning to drugs or alcohol. But hold on—God is at work!

(*Read aloud **Romans 8:28.***)

Trust this promise! Look for God at work in the midst of your trials. And because you trust God for your ultimate deliverance, there are some things you can do too:

- Do the best you can with what you have been given. Look for ways to turn "lemons" into "lemonade."
- Find a friend or mentor with whom to talk; write in a journal. Remember that God is always with you—listening and responding! Look for the signs.
- Pray for perspective; ask God to help you see the difficulty in a new light and provide a new direction. Let your trust in God override the guilt, anger, sadness, and grief that can consume you from the inside out.
- Be patient but know that God's deliverance is sure.

In the midst of your fire, God is there also. You are not alone. Let's pray.

Other Movie Options

Choose one of these or ask the youth to recommend a more recent release. Be sure to preview the selection to avoid any content that would be objectionable in your setting. Remember that you must have a video license.
(Video licensing information on CD)

- *The Princess Diaries* (2001) (the letter from her deceased father)

Leader Scripture Exploration

- **Genesis 37–46** (Joseph was betrayed, enslaved, falsely accused, imprisoned.)
- **Ruth** (Ruth lost nearly all of her family and her livelihood.)
- **Job** (Job lost nearly everything.)
- **Daniel 1:1–6:28** (Daniel and friends led an uncertain life in exile.)

Talk Tip

Arrange in advance for a team of youth to present the Bible story a dramatic form. They can act it out—live or videotaped. They can pantomime while someone reads the Scripture; they can do a reader's theatre presentation. You will find working with this team in advance gives you the opportunity for additional teachable moments as the team prepares!

On Screen

Key points in Focus Thoughts (PowerPoint® on CD)

On-the-Street Interview

What do you do when you feel like the whole world is against you?

Create-a-Video

Stage a conversation between Shadrach, Meshach, and Abednego (three volunteer youth). The setting could be before being inside the fiery furnace or afterward—perhaps, even years later, looking back.

Instead of a Message

Show a video or interview a holocaust survivor. The Internet is a helpful tool in finding these stories, printed or videotaped. Simply use a search engine and type in "holocaust survivor."

 Service Project

Have the youth group do some random acts of kindness, such as paying parking meters, picking up litter around the church or another public area, or leaving nice notes on people's cars.
(Additional idea on CD)

Youth Witness Statement

Invite a youth to talk about the experience of going through difficult times and how trust in God made a difference. (How-to on CD)

 **FoCUS GRoUP** (Additional questions on CD)

- Do you think that Shadrach, Meshach, and Abednego were sure that God would rescue them? (*Reread Daniel 3:17-18.*)
- Many Christians have faced terrible situations trusting in God's deliverance. Not all of them were rescued; some died. Does that mean that their trust in God for deliverance was misplaced? that God failed them? Is there more than one kind of "deliverance"?
- Some faithful persons have had to deal with horrible circumstances for an extended time; some, seemingly forever. In the Bible we have stories of Joseph in captivity for years and Job, who lost everything—his family, his possessions, his health. Where is God's deliverance in those circumstances? How do faithful people hang on?
- (*Reread Romans 8:28.*) What do you think it means to be "called according to God's purposes"? What are God's purposes?

CLOSING

The Consuming Fire

Have the youth continue to put the squares of paper into the locked box. This week encourage them to give to God the situations that seem too big for them to handle alone. Invite them to include situations where they have been wronged or where they knowingly wronged someone.

Fret and Worry

Shadrach, Meshach, and Abednego were unfairly subjected to what appeared to be certain death. They had no jury or court to appeal to; the king had decided. But they chose death over denying their God. They knew the one true God and trusted God even in the face of death. God protected them in the fiery furnace. They were truly delivered—not a hair on their heads was harmed. God can use the trials of our lives in surprising ways. Because of Shadrach, Meshach, and Abednego's faithfulness, God was glorified and showed true power in the face of unbelievable circumstances. God was able to touch the hearts of an entire community.

When we are determined to have our own way, we will also get worry. Jesus is never referred to throughout the Scripture as worried; he left things in the hands of God. He had his own ideas but didn't try to force them to happen. If he had, he wouldn't have died on the cross—he asked God to take it from him. We need to include God in our plans; we make the effort and then release the result to God. We can give our worry and fretting over to God. God is greater than even our toughest trial.

Fan the Flame

SOUL FOOD: Encouraging one another is one thing we can do to, in a small way, make this world better.

SCRIPTURE: 2 Timothy1:6-7 (God gives you power.)

Games

We're in This Together

Divide the youth into teams of 5–10. Assign each person a body part: eye(s), ear(s), mouth, brain, leg(s), hand(s). Give each group this challenge: With each body part performing only its function, the "body" is to "walk" over to the Bible, find Romans 12:4-6, and read it aloud. Remind the "body" that each body part may perform only its function. For example, the legs may not go until the eye tells the brain where they are and the brain tells the legs how many steps to take and in which direction to reach the Bible.

Keep the Fire Going

Divide the youth into 2 teams. Give each team a blanket and a basketball. Place a half-bushel basket or a laundry basket across the room in front of each team. On "Go," the first person on each team holds onto the basketball (the fuel) and hops onto the blanket; while the second person grabs a couple corners of the blanket and pulls the rider toward the basket (the fire). The rider has only one shot to throw the "fuel" into the "fire." The teams cheer on their players. Each time the "fuel" is successfully thrown into the "fire," that team scores a point. The game continues for a specified amount of time.

After the throw, successful or not, the two players exchange places and return to their team. The blanket does not need to move beyond the throwing spot. The puller retrieves the ball and hops onto the blanket, which is then to be pulled by the former rider.

Strategy: The rider may choose to throw the "fuel" from a distance, in which case, a successful throw could save time. However, if the throw is unsuccessful, the pair will have wasted valuable time. The rider may also choose to ride all the way up to the "fire" before placing the "fuel" into the fire. This may result in points that take longer to rack up.

SHARE AND CARE GROUPS

Checking in: Highs and lows of the week, prayer requests, and prayer

Warm up: Talk about overcoming fear. Hand out "12 Ways to Blast Away Fear" to give youth some practical help. (Handout on CD)

HAVE IT YOUR WAY!
Choose from, adapt, or rearrange these elements to create the best soul feast for your youth group.

THE FIXIN'S
More fun stuff to make the theme extra special! Your choice.

Munchies

- TNT Chili
- Mexican Cheesecake

Popular Songs

Use these before and/or after the program to engage the youth. These are some options. Try to include the latest appropriate popular songs.

- "Breakaway," by Kelly Clarkson (*Breakaway*)
- "The Flame Passes On" by White Heart (*Highlands*)
- "Burn the Ships," Steven Curtis Chapman (*Heaven in the Real World*)
- "Proud Mary" Tina Turner (*What's Love Got to Do With It?*)
- "Achy Breaky Heart," by Billy Ray Cyrus (*Some Gave All*)
- "Jail House Rock," by Elvis (*Elvis: 30 #1 Hits*)

Worship and Praise Music

- "As the Deer"
- "Change My Heart, O God"
- "Here I Am to Worship," by Tim Hughes (*Worship Together: Here I Am to Worship*)
- "Eternally Grateful," by Chris Newman (*Tarp Town Years*)
- "Consuming Fire," by Third Day (*Offerings: A Worship Album*)

On-the-Street Interviews

• What would you do to encourage someone around you?
• What was the nicest thing someone has done to encourage you?

Out and About

Go rock climbing or rappelling. Be sure to have the appropriate safety equipment and instruction. The goal for the experience is to have everyone successfully complete the challenge. Keep the focus on encouraging one another. Afterward, talk about how the encouragement from the group helped. Ask what the experience would have been like if persons in the group were not encouraging or were even disparaging.

Youth Group Rule

Some youth groups have a "no put-down policy." Even when meant in fun, a put-down has a sting that lasts. So whenever anyone slips on the rule, he or she (youthworker included) has to stop and say three complimentary things to the person who was the recipient of the offending remark. Encourage, encourage, encourage!

Focus Point

Video Option: *The Princess Diaries* (2001) (Start: 40:16; stop: 42:24 or 43:28) has several scenes where her mother or her grandmother encourages her, I particularly like the scene where she has her hair straightened and her limo driver/security agent gives her some encouragement after she suffers criticism from her friend, Lily. Be sure to preview your selection to avoid any content that would be objectionable in your setting. Remember that you must have a video license. (Video licensing information on CD)

Skit Option: **Helpful/Not Helpful** (Directions on CD)

Focus Thoughts (Text on CD)

Simply encouraging one another is one of the most overlooked things we can do to make this world a better place. One small thing you say or do can have a dramatic impact on someone's day—or life. Your encouragement and support may help someone get through a really hard day, perhaps even giving him or her the strength to go on living. When you build up people, you are laying a foundation for them to become the kind of persons who, in turn, build up others, perhaps even as world leaders. We never quite know the power of our words and actions. We can, however, choose to use that power with love.

We all need one another. As Christians, we are connected as "the body of Christ" in ways that encourage and support us. Because we are blessed with God's love, we then can be a blessing to others. Finding ways to make others' lives better, helping people in need, sharing God's love will fan the flame of your life and the lives of others—especially those right around you.

Optional: Today we will be taking all of the papers we have filled out that are in the locked box and burning them. We all need to let go of the past and start focusing on the present and the future. Remembering trials, pain, hurt, bad decisions is good helping us to keep from making the same mistakes again; but it isn't good for moving forward into the future. (Get the locked box.) That is why we are going to use the symbol of fire to clean up the old and make way for the new at the end of the session.

Imagine that you could take back all of the negative things you have ever said, done, believed, or thought and start over. How would you feel if all of those things simply never happened? We would all feel a sense of freedom and happiness. God is willing and able to take on whatever bad stuff is weighing us down. Jesus died to free us from the power of sin—all that bad stuff. When we ask for forgiveness, God gives us a new beginning and a new kind of power.

(*Read aloud* ***2 Timothy 1:6-7.***)

Fear, timidity, cowardice do not come from God. Rekindle—fan into flame—the gift of God that is within you. God is offering you a spirit of power, love, and self-discipline. Use that power and love to bless those around you. The simplest of ways is to be an encourager. Go and do it! Let's pray.

FOCUS GROUP (Questions on CD)

- How do you feel when you are criticized? When you are encouraged?
- What do you think forgiveness offers us?
- What is freedom in Christ?
- What are some simple ways to encourage those around you?

CLOSING (Alternative closing, "I Will . . . ," on CD)

Circle of Encouragement

Have each youth sit in the center chair in a circle of chairs. The person must sit there for one to two minutes while the other members of the group continually feed him or her encouragement. If the group does not know the person in the center well, have them say things that start with "You look like a person who…" or "God loves you."

The Consuming Fire

Take the group and the locked box outside to a grill or fire pit. Burn the papers a few at a time. Burn all the past sorrows, things that the youth feel that they need forgiveness for, the habits they want to break, and so on. As you do, read aloud **Hebrews 12:28:**

> "Therefore, since we are receiving a kingdom that cannot be shaken, let us give thanks, by which we offer to God an acceptable worship with reverence and awe; for indeed our God is a consuming fire."

Remind the youth that we offer our failings, our sorrows to God and God consumes them. They become ash and blow away; there is nothing left of them. Notice that there is no longer a record of these failings or sorrows, and God won't bring them up again! We are forgiven!

Invite youth to pray silently. Close by singing "Awesome God" or another appropriate and familiar song.

Youth Witness Statement

Invite a youth to talk about the experience of going through difficult times and how the encouragement of others made a difference.
(How-to on CD)

IT Takes Two (OR MORE)

WE'RE IN THIS TOGETHER

From the beginning, God did not create one person—God created two! We are to be in relationship with one another—and with God. Examine with the youth what makes healthy relationships with their parents, friends, boyfriends or girlfriends, and God.

APPETIZERS (Additional ideas on CD)

Publicity Ideas: *Here are some fun ideas for whetting the appetite of your youth! Some are particular to one of the programs; others are more general.*

Use the theme logo to create posters, flyers, and/or postcards. Include the dates, time, and location.

Print out the Best Friends Necklace (Design on CD) as a large poster. Or make a large "Best Friends" necklace from butcher paper and hang it on the wall. Make sure to include the date, time, and location of your meeting about relationships with friends.

☺ **Invite-a-Friend Night:** Have the youth invite their friends to youth group the night you discuss friendships. You can give a small prize like a mini candy bars to everyone who brings a friend, or offer a prize to the person who brings the most friends. Either way, make sure that you have enough candy for the friends too.

☺ **Kissing Booth:** Set up a kissing booth that hands out Hershey Kisses and Hugs®, with slips of paper containing the date and time of the lesson on relationships with boyfriends or girlfriends.

☺ **Flower Delivery:** During the youth group, have flowers delivered to yourself or to one of the youth. Have someone read aloud the card that came with the flowers. On the card is the info inviting youth to the meeting where you'll discuss relationships with boyfriends and girlfriends. Since flower shops may not be open during youth group hours, buy flowers from a grocery store and keep them hidden until the appropriate time. Have one of the other youth leaders come in to the room with the flowers and interrupt saying, "These were just delivered for. . . ." Another option is to do a balloon bouquet, instead of flowers.

☺ **Life Saver:** Wear water wings, a life vest, or a life saver ring (or all three for more fun); and ask the youth, "What will save your life?" Invite the youth to the lesson on relationships with God to find out how to save their life.

DRINKS

" 'Lord, when was it that we saw you . . . thirsty and gave you something to drink? . . .' 'Truly, I tell you, just as you did it to one of the least of these' " (Matthew 25:37, 40a).

Service project ideas

COMBOS MENU

Main Dishes

Weekly Program Options: *Choose one or all; do in any order. Check each description for variations and the fixin's. Invite a team of youth to plan with you.*

1. **Parents Just Don't Understand**—That's a familiar complaint among teens. But here's an opportunity to take a fresh look at what's behind parent weirdness—and may be even to fix it.

2. **I'll Be There for You**—We all count on our friends, but how do we become the kind of person they can count on?

3. **This Could Be Contagious**—A special boyfriend or girlfriend in our life makes us feel great. But there are some ground rules needed to keep the relationship and the individuals healthy.

4. **God, Not Gaud** —Often we're so busy trying to do all the right things to be successful by the world's standards that we lose sight of truc success and forget to trust God. God is God—not just a showy ornament for display when convenient.

Spice It Up

Theme Decorations: *Let your space add to the discussion. Change the look each week for the different topics.*

- **Parents:** Placc enlarged parent and youth baby pictures around the youth room or church. Also use parents' middle school or high school yearbook pictures. Make life-sized posterboard cutouts of parents' high school photos and place them around the room. For added fun, take instant or digital pictures with the cutouts. (Link to FedEx Kinko's website on CD)

- **Friends:** Try to make the youth area look like the places where youth like to hang out (coffee shop, living room, mall, and so forth).

- **Boyfriends/Girlfriends:** Decorate the youth room with heart shapes cut from red and pink construction paper. Create mood lighting; dim the lights for that romantic feel. Play cheesy, romantic music—the cornier the better.

- **God:** Create cotton clouds and put them around the youth room. If you have access to dry ice, create some special effects that make the youth room seem like a distant place in the clouds. You'll need a small fan to help spread the fog along the floor.

Parents Just Don't Understand

Have It Your Way!

Choose from, adapt, or rearrange these elements to create the best soul feast for your youth group.

The Fixin's

More fun stuff to make the theme extra special! Your choice.

Munchies

- Sugar Daddy® candy
- Dad's® root beer floats
- Popsicles®
- Mother's Cookies®
- Mama Ella's of Hawaii® cookies
- Have parents bring favorite treats from home.

Invite Parents

If having parents will keep youth from being honest and speaking up, split the parents off into another room for their own small groups. Modify the questions slightly. Have both groups come together for the talk and closing.

Popular Songs

Use these before and/or after the program to engage the youth. These are some options. Try to include the latest appropriate popular songs.

- "Lean on Me," by Bill Withers (*Lean on Me—The Best of Bill Withers*)
- "In My Daughter's Eyes," by Martina McBride (*Martina*)
- "Drive (for Daddy Gene)," by Alan Jackson (*Greatest Hits, Volume II*)
- "Everything I Own," by Bread (*The Best of Bread*)
- "Parents Just Don't Understand," by DJ Jazzy Jeff and the Fresh Prince (*Jazzy Jeff and Fresh Prince—Greatest Hits*)
- Any songs by The Mommas & the Papas

SOUL FOOD: By honoring our parents, we may find that they increasingly honor us as well.

SCRIPTURE: Exodus 20:12 (Honor your parents.) Ephesians 6:1-4 (Parents honor your children.)

Games (Additional games on CD)

Parents Say the Darndest Things

Divide the youth into teams of four or five. Have each team list weird, annoying and/or "dumb" things their parents say. This can include sayings that parents use over and over, bits of "wisdom" parents repeat, or, even a once-in-a-lifetime (we hope!) spewing of something that made no sense at all. Set a time limit, then have all the groups tell what they have listed. For added fun, have youth deliver the lines in the same tone and manner as a parent would. (Create-a-Video option on CD)

Mother, May I

In this classic game, participants must precede every request with, "Mother, May I...." Have one, or however many youth you choose, play "Mother" while the remaining youth try to reach the goal line and become "Mother" (or "Father," as appropriate). Reward those who make it to "parenthood."

Share and Care Groups

Checking in: Highs and lows of the week, prayer requests, and prayer

Warm up: Have the group make one list of things about which youth and parents often agree, and another list of things on which parents and youth usually disagree. Use categories such as curfew, dating, movies, TV shows, friends, styles of clothes, music, homework. (Alternative ideas on CD)

Focus Point

Video Option: *Finding Nemo* (2003) (Start: 0:00; stop: 10:56—"For a clown fish, he really isn't that funny." "Pity.") Nemo is the only family that his father, Marlin, has left. Like most parents, Marlin is pretty nervous about all the things that may (or may not) happen to his son when he starts school.

Skit Option: In advance of the meeting, give this scenario to two to four youth to create and present a skit about all-too-typical communication between parents and teens. (Scenario on CD)

⊙ Focus Thoughts (Text on CD)

Why are parents the way they are? They can be weird, irrational, embarrassing, and strange. But are parents as bad as they seem? And is it really all *their* fault? Could we be contributing to the situations that cause our parents to freak-out, pester us with questions, and butt into our business. (Refer to the Focus Point skit if you used it, or just describe the scenario.)

You may feel like you're "reporting in" when you have to tell your parents the details of your life. But do you think parents are really just trying to make you miserable? Or could it be that they're concerned about you?

Of course, some of you have done things that give your parents good reason to be worried. (Haven't you?) Some of your parents are justified in asking questions about your plans. But for the most part, when your parents ask questions, it's because they're uninformed and feel uncomfortable. So try to answer their questions and give them the info they need to feel more comfortable, then it won't seem like they are invading your privacy or always hounding you for more info. Besides, if you're lying to your parents about what you're doing, should you really be doing it?

Believe it or not, your parents did many of the same things you do when you're with friends. Parents may seem old and out-of-touch; but in reality, they were once "typical" teenagers just like you. Parents often know what kind of things you're up to, and many of them have had bad experiences as a result of doing those same things. Parents in their hard-to-understand ways might actually be trying to protect you from similar experiences.

OK, so there are some legitimate times when parents go overboard. They upset us, get on our nerves, and act in ways we can't explain. But for the most part, parents don't mean to be annoying; they're just being parents.

Let's think about things from a parent's perspective for a moment. Even before you were born, you were already a part of your parents' life for nine or so months. You had a dramatic impact on their lives—and you weren't even born yet! After you were born, you were totally dependent on your parents. Slowly, you started becoming your own person, but you still needed Mom or Dad to kiss boo-boos. You continued to turn to them for protection, guidance, comfort, and security. They taught you important lessons, such as look both ways before crossing the street and don't get into a car with a stranger.

As you grew, you developed your own likes and dislikes, established priorities, and formed opinions. You tried sports, playing musical instruments, Scouts, arts, and all sorts of things. You became a capable young person, relying less and less on your parents. One day, usually around middle school, you began experiencing the wild ride of crazy hormones. For the most part, your parents were the last ones you wanted to talk to about this. So you clammed up, and not communicating drives you and your parents farther away from each other.

Soon you were a very capable teenager. You started to get that guy/girl hormone thing under control. And now for the most part, you feel good about yourself and confident. You rely less on your parents now. They provide a house to live in, food to eat, maybe a car to get around in,; and occasionally they slip you a few extra bucks. But when it comes to personal things and social matters, you handle them on your own. Once you're sixteen with your driver's license, you don't even need them to drive you around anymore. In a very short time, you have become mostly independent. You no longer need or

Worship and Praise Music

- "Father I Adore You" (*25 Praise and Worship Songs You Love to Sing*)
- "Abba Father," by Rebecca St. James (*Wow 1998: The Year's 30 Top Christian Artists and Songs*)
- "Big House," Audio Adrenaline (*Hit Parade*)

⊙ Other Movie Options

Choose one of these movies, or ask the youth to recommend a more recent release. Be sure to preview your selection to avoid any content that would be objectionable in your setting. Remember that you must have a video license.
(Video licensing information on CD)

Big Fish (2004)
Stepmom (1998)
Freaky Friday (2003)
Bill Cosby, Himself (1983)

On-the-Street Interviews (Ideas on CD)

Consult the CD for a pair of ideas that can be used for the Focus Point or the Closing or as "bookends" for both. These can be videotaped.

⊙ Leader Scripture Exploration

- **Proverbs 6:20-22** (The teachings of your parents will guide you and watch over you.)
- **Ephesians 4:29-32** (Paul lists rules for getting along with one another as Christians.)
- **Colossians 3:20-21** (Paul gives instructions to parents and children.)

Talk Tips

Include personal stories to illustrate how, when growing up, you experienced some of the same things with your parents that youth are currently experiencing with theirs.

Pose questions in the talk and invite students to respond, making the talk more like an interactive discussion than a lecture.

💿 Out and About

Hold the meeting in a family counselor's office. You can even invite the counselor to sit in and offer insight at the end.
(Additional ideas on CD)

Service Projects

Arrange for a parent and youth nursing home visit, mission trip, soup kitchen help, and so forth. Any outreach service project that is done together will enhance the relationship between youth and parents.

Announcement Ideas

Have a youth dress, talk, and act like a parent to make an announcement at youth group, telling everyone about the upcoming lesson on parent youth relationships. The more exaggerated and stereotypical the youth acts the better!

Or for real laughs and a sight that youth will remember for a long time, have parents dress, talk, and act like youth to make the announcement. Again, the more exaggerated the better!

💿 Youth Witness Statement

Have a youth who has studied abroad, or spent an extended period of time away from his or her family give a witness statement about how important those parent relationships are, especially when you're out on your own. (How-to on CD)

want Mom and Dad in the same way you did before. Here's where you have to look from the parent perspective: Parents feel you pulling away and becoming your own person; they feel less and less needed as you go from total dependence on them to wanting total independence from them.

Now, parents have a tough job here. They are excited about the possibilities that lie ahead for you as you mature. But at the same time, that means that they have to let go more and more, which is one of the hardest things for them to do. This battle between holding on and letting go is waging within your parents; sometimes you get caught in the middle of the war zone.

Here's another secret that you already know but that parents don't like to admit: Parents are not experts. Each parenting situation is unique. Each child is different; and parents try to address each child in an effective way, not necessarily with the same approach. Parents learn from one experience, which sometimes helps them with the next—and sometimes it doesn't. Do you know where first-time parents get their parenting knowledge? They can get a little from reading books or taking classes, but the majority of their knowledge comes from their own memories and experiences growing up. They look to their parents' example. So when you're mad at your parents for the way they act in certain situations, you can blame your grandmas and grandpas. And when you become a parent for the first time, guess where you're going to turn for an example? Your parents!

Let's look at Scripture. Of course, you recognize the fifth commandment.

(*Read aloud Exodus 20:12.*)

Of course, it takes two to make a great relationship.

(*Read aloud Ephesians 6:1-4.*)

God also calls parents to respect and not discourage their children. However, like us, parents are human too. They have mixed-up feelings to deal with, and they make their share of mistakes. We may not agree with all their decisions; we may not like how they handle situations. But for the most part, they are expressing their love and concern for us.

God calls us to honor our parents. We can do that by looking at things from a parent perspective, recognizing their love and concern for us, giving them what they need to feel confident in us, and being more forgiving toward them. In honoring them, we may well discover that they are increasingly honoring us, as well. After all, it takes two for a great relationship. Let's pray.

 **FOCUS GROUP** (Additional questions on CD)

- What are your reactions to the talk? What new ideas did you get from it?
- In what ways are you already consistently honoring your parents?
- Since relationships are two-way streets, what can you do, or what are you going to do, to change and improve one relationship at home?

 **CLOSING** (Additional ideas on CD)

Prayer Circle

Have everyone form a circle; focus on prayers for parents and youth. Go around the circle or pick youth at random—it doesn't matter how you do it,. It just matters that you do it. If parents are present at the meeting, form the circle of youth around them and pray for them while they stand in the middle.

I'LL BE THERE FOR YOU

SOUL FOOD: Making God the center of our lives also makes us into the kind of person who is a good friend.

SCRIPTURE: Philippians 2:3-5a (Consider the interests of others as well as of yourself.)

GAMES (Additional games on CD)

Human Knot

This is knot your ordinary game. In a group of five or more, facing toward the center, players reach into the group and randomly grab hands with two other people. Once everyone is connected, they begin untangling the knot without breaking the connections. Don't give up. It is possible to do this. This is a great exercise in working together, listening, and getting along.

Body Part Match Up

When the leader calls out a number and a body part, players race to get into groups of that number and touch the designated body parts together in the center of the group. For example, if the leader calls out "7 pinky fingers," players would race to get into groups of seven with each player holding a pinky finger into the middle. Mix up the quantity and body parts called: feet, ears, fingers, hips, elbows heels, shoulders. You can choose to have players not in a group be "out" and have to wait for the next game, leading to the eventual "winners" when only two people are left. Or so that everyone is included throughout, you can just play for fun with nobody having to be out of the game.

SHARE AND CARE GROUPS

Checking in: Each person tells one good thing and one not-so-good thing that happened with their friends over the past week. Close this time with prayer, asking members of the group whether they have a specific friend or friendship that needs prayer. If mentioning this out loud in front of the group is intimidating for them, try breaking the group into pairs and have the youth pray for each other's friends.

Warm up: Have the group create a list of qualities they look for in a friend. Then have them think of one or two specific friends. As you read through the master list, have the youth make a mental note of which qualities their friends possess and which ones they are lacking. Then ask youth which qualities they think they have and which ones they need to work on developing.

Have It Your Way!

Choose from, adapt, or rearrange these elements to create the best soul feast for your youth group.

The Fixin's

More fun stuff to make the theme extra special! Your choice.

Munchies

- Friendship Tea
- Go to a Friendly's restaurant if you have that chain in your area.
- Look for an eating establishment offering two-for-one, or buy-one, get-one-free deals. Check the coupons in your entertainment book or slick sections of your newspaper. Then have youth take their friend out for a meal or snack.
- Serve Oreo® cookies and milk—a classic snack to share with a friend.

Popular Songs

Use these before and/or after the program to engage the youth. These are some options. Try to include the latest appropriate popular songs.

- "You've Got a Friend," by James Taylor (*The Best of James Taylor*)
- "You've Got a Friend in Me," by Randy Newman with Lyle Lovett (*Toy Story: An Original Walt Disney Record's Soundtrack*)
- "Lean on Me," by Bill Withers (*Lean on Me—The Best of Bill Withers*)
- "I'll be There for You," by The Rembrandts (*LP*)
- "Promise," by When in Rome (*When in Rome*)

Worship and Praise Music

- "Friends," by Michael W. Smith (*The First Decade: 1983–1993*)
- "He Ain't Heavy ... He's My Brother," by Neil Diamond (*Gold*)
- "I Can Be Your Friend," by The OC Supertones (*Veggie Rocks*)

Other Movie Options

Choose one of these movies, or ask students to recommend a more recent release. Be sure to preview your selection to avoid any content that would be objectionable in your setting. Remember that you must have a video license.
(Video licensing information on CD)

- *Toy Story* (1995)
- *Mean Girls* (2004)—Show especially the "Queen Bees and Wannabes" feature in DVD bonus material.
- *Star Wars* (1997) *Show the final battle scene, when Han Solo shows up and saves Luke, who in turn saves the day. Talk about friends doing things for each other and putting their friends before themselves.*
- *Remember the Titans* (2000)

Leader Exploration Scripture

- **Proverbs 13:20** (Who your companions are makes a difference.)
- **John 15:12-14** (Love one another.)

Talk Tips

Have a youth or two tell a personal story about an adventure with a best friend.

On-the-Street Interviews

Videotape kids' responses to questions like, "What quality do you admire most in a friend?"
(Additional ideas on CD)

Focus Point

Video Options: *Napoleon Dynamite* (2004) (Start: 1:16:25, the crowd applauds as Summer walks across the stage; stop: 1:23:23, the cheering stops) This story takes place in a small rural town in Idaho and focuses on high school student Napoleon Dynamite and the relationships in his life. One of the most important relationships is his friendship with Pedro Sanchez. Pedro is running for student body president against the most popular girl in school. At the last minute, Pedro learns that he must present a skit following his speech, but he has nothing planned. As a true friend, Napoleon steps in to help his friend Pedro. The alternative ending (1:26) shows the "happy ending" to each of the relationships in the movie including Napoleon and Deb.

Friendship Jewelry Options: (Ideas and instructions on CD)

Focus Thoughts (Text and original version on CD)

Do you have a best friend with whom you can talk to about anything? Let me tell you about my best friend when I was in high school. (*Tell the youth about your best friend, whether it was back in high school, college, or as a young adult. Relate a story or two that illustrates why you were such good friends. Tell about some adventure the two of you shared. Also talk about what role Christ and your faith played in the friendship. Follow the story through so that the youth know what happened in that friendship. Are you still friends? Have you lost track of each other? Do you keep in touch once in a while?*)

It's important to have a close friend, someone to share with and to confide in, someone to support you and hold you accountable. Likewise, it's important to have someone who confides in you, someone for you to hold accountable, someone who can count on you to "be there."

(*Share your experience growing up and the friends you had. Did you move a lot or live in the same place your whole life? Did you have a bunch of friends, a couple close friends, one best friend, or many best friends? And do you see your experience as a plus or minus in developing friendships? Are you a better friend because of your experiences growing up?*)

Friendships can last a lifetime; and unfortunately some friendships will die out. Friends will come and go. Some you will know for a short time, and others you may know a lifetime. One way to make all of your friendships stronger and more meaningful is to include God.

What does it mean to "include God" in a friendship? One aspect is simply to acknowledge God's importance, to be free to talk about your faith with your friend, to make decisions together based on faith, to be comfortable enough to pray for each other and with each other.

Scripture gives us insight into another aspect of what it means to "include God" in a friendship.

(*Read aloud **Philippians 2:3-5a**.*)

When we follow the example and teachings of Jesus, we become persons of love, not conceited or self-absorbed; but the person who looks to the interests of others, not just our own. That's the kind of friend anyone would want. That is the basis for a strong and loving friendship. Let's pray.

 **F⊚CUS GR⊚UP** <u>(Additional questions on CD)</u>

- How do the church and youth group help you to be a good friend?
- Do you talk to your friends about your faith or about God? If yes, what do you talk about? If no, why not?
- How are Christian friends different from non-Christian friends?
- What role does God play in your friendships with church friends, and with non-church friends?
- Around non-Christian friends, do you hide your faith? And can you truly be yourself around non-Christian friends? What about differences in morals and ethics; who compromises?
- Specifically, how can God bring one of your friendships closer?

CL⊚SING <u>(Additional idea and resource on CD)</u>

Group Hugs

Do the **traditional method** where the group simply moves toward someone in the center of a circle, stay in an expanded circle with arms interlaced over one another's shoulders.

Or try the **"cinnamon roll sticky bun hug."** Line the group up in a single-file line, holding hands. Starting at one end of the line, have the youth roll into the line toward the opposite end of the line. As youth twist they will add more and more people until the entire line is rolled into a cinnamon-roll shape. The first person is now at the center of the sticky bun. Be careful during this one not to get dizzy.

Pray for a Friend

During closing prayer, have each youth pray for one of his or her friends or a friendship that needs healing. Encourage the youth to move beyond just praying for a friend who has a test in math this week and to pray for sincere matters relating to their friendships.

Friendship Blessing <u>(Worship service on CD)</u>

Create a Video

Go to teenagers' schools, sports events, the mall, or any other place where youth hang out. Videotape youth from the group with their friends. Some youth may be surprised to see how they behave around their friends. It will also be interesting to see whether they act differently around their youth-group friends than they do around their non-youth-group friends.

Out and About

Do this lesson at a local middle school or high school campus. If there is a teacher in your church, ask whether your group may meet in his or her classroom. Have the youth give "tours" of their school, pointing out where their locker is, where they eat lunch, where they usually hang out with friends.
<u>(Additional ideas on CD)</u>

Service Projects

- <u>Secret Pals</u>
- <u>Invite a Friend to Serve</u>

Youth Witness Statements

- Have a youth tell about the important role a friend has played in his or her life, perhaps how that friend helped him or her overcome something such as a divorce, a parent dying, a personal illness or illness in the family, a break-up with a girlfriend or boyfriend. Focus on the positive influence of the friendship and not the hardship.

- Have a youth give a witness statement about why Christian friendships are important and how Christian friendships have had an impact on his or her life.
<u>(How-to on CD)</u>

THIS COULD BE CONTAGIOUS

Have It Your Way!

Choose from, adapt, or rearrange these elements to create the best soul feast for your youth group.

The Fixin's

More fun stuff to make the theme extra special! Your choice.

 Munchies

- Set out bowls of Hershey's Kisses and Hugs™.
- Make <u>Heart-Shaped Sugar Cookies</u> or brownies with heart-shaped sprinkles.

Popular Songs

Use these before and/or after the program to engage the youth. These are some options. Try to include the latest appropriate popular songs.

- "I Wanna Hold Your Hand," by the Beatles (*The Beatles 1*)
- "Hello, I Love You," by The Doors (*The Best of The Doors*)
- "The Rose," by Bette Midler (*Greatest Hits—Experience the Divine*)

Worship and Praise Music

- "Open the Eyes of My Heart," by Paul Baloche (*Open the Eyes of My Heart*)

SOUL FOOD: Dating can be a very positive experience when the ground rules are based on God's rules.

SCRIPTURE: 1 Thessalonians 4:3-5 (Learn to control your own body in a way that is holy and honorable.)

Games (Additional games on CD)

Baby, If You Love Me, Smile

Have the youth sit on chairs in a circle. The player who is "It" approaches someone and says, "Baby, if you love me, smile." Without smiling, that person must respond, "Baby, I love you; but I just can't smile." If the person smiles, he or she becomes It. If a player successfully responds without smiling, he or she is safe; and It must make another attempt with a different player. After three failed attempts, It may choose a replacement.

To get a person to smile, It may sit on someone's lap, kneel beside or in front of the player, twirl a finger in the player's hair while whispering sweet nothings into his or her ear. But It may not tickle anyone to get a smile.

Lifesaver Pass

Here's a game where you won't get slapped for "making a pass" at someone. Divide the youth into teams of equal numbers, giving each person a toothpick. Each team also needs a LifeSavers® candy. Players hold the toothpick in their mouth while standing in a single-file line. The object of the game is to pass the candy from the front to the back of the line, without dropping it or using hands. Place the candy on the toothpick of the person first in line.

When the leader says go, teams start passing candy from player to player. If the candy falls or is touched by hands, pick it up and begin again from the front of the line. The first team to complete the task wins.

As an alternative, give each team a pack of LifeSavers® and see how many candies each team can pass through the line in a set amount of time. If you have only enough youth for one team, use a race-the-clock option.

Share and Care Groups

Checking in: Highs and lows of the week, prayer requests, and prayer

Warm up: Make a choice. Give copies of the instructions and questions to your small group leaders. (<u>Questions on CD</u>)

FꝊCUS PꝊint

Video Option: *50 First Dates* As a heads-up, there is a rude gesture included in the following clip. (Start: 1:25, "Lucy…"; stop: 1:31, when the walruses kiss.) Henry Roth (Adam Sandler) is a marine biologist working at a sea-park in Hawaii. Roth enjoys a carefree life of one-night stands with female tourists looking for an island fling. One day, Roth meets Lucy (Drew Barrymore), an island resident and the fun begins. Lucy, having suffered a head injury in a car accident, has no long-term memory. Every night when she sleeps, the previous day's memories fade. Roth is tireless in his efforts to make Lucy fall in love with him all over again each day. Use this clip to show how romantic love between people can't be selfish. Roth loves Lucy so much that he makes a video for her to watch each morning; Roth is willing to "start over" every day. His love for her overcomes her lack of memory.

Activity Option: Mr. & Ms. Perfect—Have each youth cut from magazines and newspapers any words and images of people that describe, represent, and show their idea of the perfect guy or girl. Then the youth will show their creation to the group. Or, instead of this being an individual project, the whole group may create a collage with multiple images that represent the group's idea of the perfect guy or girl. When it is finished, have youth discuss their creation. Ask the creators what was important to them in making their choices. Was it looks, brains, athletic ability, musical talents, social standing, wealth, emotions or something else?

FꝊCUS THꝊUGHtS (Text on CD)

Dating can be pretty awkward at times. I mean, just wondering whether someone likes you is hard. There's this person you like, so you have your friends ask that person's friends whether that person likes you. Or when you were younger, you would write a note to the person; and it would have, "Do you like me? Check below." And you had a box for "YES," and a box for "NO," and a box for "MAYBE." Ah, those were the days! A relationship established or a heart broken—with a piece of paper and a checked box!

Then there's the first date. Why is it that when you're getting ready for that first date and you're all excited, you look good, you dress nice, then you walk into the bathroom, look in the mirror, and on your face is a what? (A big-time zit!) Talk about embarrassing! Well, pimples come and go. First dates come and go. And boyfriends and girlfriends come and go.

So why do we even have boyfriends and girlfriends? Why do we put ourselves through those emotional ups and downs? Why are we so driven by the opposite sex? The answer is simple—because God made us that way. God created us male and female with a natural attraction to one another.

So if this is God's design and God wants us to be attracted to each other, why do we have to keep ourselves under control? Why can't we just give in and go wild with the gift God put in us?

Some people do go wild and take advantage of the gift of sexuality. We frequently hear about the sexual conquests of professional athletes and rock stars, but we don't have to look to famous people for examples of abusing God's gift. You probably know people at your school who are having sex. Some of you may be abusing God's gift by engaging in those same activities. But listen to what the Bible says in **1 Thessalonians 4:3-5:**

Note: Because of the topic of sex, many movie possibilities may have some scenes that are inappropriate for viewing. There are some scenes within these suggestions, however, that, if viewed and chosen ahead, are appropriate and can be helpful in the program.

Choose one or more of the movies listed, or ask thee youth to recommend a more recent release. Be sure to preview your selection to avoid any content that would be objectionable in your setting. Remember that you must have a video license.
(Video licensing information on CD)

- *How to Lose a Guy in 10 Days* (2003)
- *The Princess Bride* (1987)

Talk Tips (Tips on CD)

Leader Scripture Exploration

- **Genesis 2:20-22** (God creates woman.)
- **1 Corinthians 6:18-20** (Your body is a temple; you were bought at a price.)
- **Ephesians 4:29-32** (Build up others; avoid what tears down.)
- **Ephesians 5:1-5** (For Christians, there should be not even a hint of sexual immorality.)

Create a Video

Recreate a relationship game show, such as *The Dating Game, Blind Date, The Newlywed Game, Elimidate, Shipmates,* or *Love Connection.*
(Additional information on CD)

On-the-Street Interviews

Interview youth and adults, asking questions such as:

- What do you like most in a guy or girl?
- What is the biggest irritation when it comes to dating?
- Can you still be friends after you break up?

Out and About

Have the group visit a marriage counselor or relationship specialist and have the counselor talk about the most common areas of conflict he or she sees in relationships. If it's doable, have your meeting in his or her office and maybe even come up with some scenarios to roleplay while you're there. This would be even better if the specialist is a Christian counselor who can add God into the equation.

Go Gender Specific

Consider dividing the youth into groups of all guys and all girls for discussion time.

Youth Witness Statement

Have youth speak about their experiences dating Christians and non-Christians. What was the impact or effect on their faith?
(Additional idea on CD)

Poster

God thinks you are special. You deserve someone special. Be choosy.
(Design on CD)

"It is God's will that you should be sanctified [which means "holy"]: that you should avoid sexual immorality; that each of you should learn to control [your] own body in a way that is holy and honorable, not in passionate lust like the heathen, who do not know God" (NIV).

The reason we can't just go "hog-wild" with our sexuality is that this gift from God has more to it than physical attraction. Sexuality comes with emotional, mental, and spiritual elements, in addition to the physical. That is why God wants us to share our sexuality only in the context of marriage. Marriage is the only relationship that is designed to fully embrace and support all of the elements of our sexuality. God is not trying to keep us from having fun. God is giving us a perfect way to share our sexuality, which can also protect us from the hurt that can come when we're overwhelmed or in a relationship that can't handle the realities of sexuality.

So why date? Why have boyfriends or girlfriends? Unfortunately, much of the world tells us that it's for physical satisfaction. But that's not what God intended. Physical gratification by itself is selfish; whereas truly loving relationships are not self-centered. They build up both persons involved.

Dating is an important part of your life. It is a chance for you to learn and grow, a chance to have an intimate (nonsexual) relationship with someone special. It's also a chance to discover what you like and dislike in a person, a chance to explore different types of people and personalities. Sometimes you like someone more than that person likes you. You work through those times, you learn from them, and life continues.

One of the hardest things about being in a special relationship is not getting caught up in the physical aspect. "Learn to control [your] own body in a way that is holy and honorable." Date when you are ready, and be choosy. Date only people who will respect you and your views on sexuality. You are a special person, God says so. You deserve someone special. That's what I mean by "be choosy." Don't rush in just because your friends are dating. Talk to your parents (yeah, right) and be in prayer with God about your dating relationships. Let's pray.

(See "Talk Tips" on CD.)

FOCUS GROUP (Additional questions on CD)

- Do your parents have restrictions on your dating? What are some of them? What do you think about these restrictions?
- What is so important about going out with someone? Is it social status?
- Is it OK to *not* have a boyfriend of girlfriend? Why, or why not?
- Is it important to have a boyfriend or girlfriend who is a Christian? What about possible differences in moral and ethical standards?

CLOSING (Additional ideas on CD)

Blessing Our Relationships

Have the youth brainstorm ways that God can be a part of their dating relationships. Then close in prayer, asking God to bless current and future dating relationships and inviting God to be an active part of those relationships.

GOD, NOt GAUD

SOUL FOOD: In our lives we can easily relegate God to the role of showy ornament (gaud); but it is being in close relationship with God that brings us abundant life.

SCRIPTURE: Matthew 6:31-33 (Seek first the kingdom of God)

**GAMES** (Additional game on CD)

Human Chess

Using tape, mark out squares on the floor to create a giant chess board. Print off small sheets of paper that contain the name, starting position and a description of movement for each piece on the board. Have youth pick pieces of paper from a hat and get into starting position on the giant board. Then have two people—adults or youth—play each other in chess by moving their players around the board. Use real chess rules. If you don't have enough youth for all of the positions, limit the number of pawns, or just get rid of the pawns all together.

Moving People

From a theater sport popularized on *Whose Line Is It, Anyway?* this fun improvisation game is played by having volunteers play the role of people while other volunteers control their movements. Another volunteer narrates the action, making up a story to match the actions of the people. The secret to this one is to keep changing the people's positions.

SHARE AND CARE GROUPS

Checking in: Highs and lows of the week, prayer requests, and prayer

Warm up: If you played Human Chess, Moving People, or Blindfold Relay (from the CD), ask the youth to tell how it felt to be controlled and told what to do all the time. Ask whether they liked the game.

Have the youth work as a group or as individuals to create a list of the top 10 priorities in their life right now. If they don't have 10 priorities, have them list as many as they can. When the youth are finished, have them tell what they put on their lists and note similarities and differences between the lists. Where was God on their lists?

Finish your Share and Care group time by asking, "If you were God for one minute, what would you do with that power?"

HAVE It YOUR WAY!

Choose from, adapt, or rearrange these elements to create the best soul feast for your youth group.

THE FIXIN'S

More fun stuff to make the theme extra special! Your choice.

Munchies

• Tootsie Pops® or Blow Pops® (What's in the center of your life?)
• Fig bars or fig cookies
• Swiss Cheese ("holy" food)

Popular Songs

Use these before and/or after the program to engage the youth. These are some options. Try to include the latest appropriate popular songs.

• "What if God Was One of Us?" by Joan Osborne (*Relish*)
• "I Love You This Much" by Billy Ray Cyrus (*The Other Side*)
• "Lean on Me," by Bill Withers (*Lean on Me—The Best of Bill Withers*)
• "Shinny Happy People," by R.E.M. (*Out of Time*)

Worship and Praise Music

• "Big House," Audio Adrenaline (*Hit Parade*)
• "I Can Only Imagine," by MercyMe (*Almost There*)
• "I Want to Know You (In the Secret)," by SonicFlood (*Gold*)
• "Open the Eyes of My Heart," by Paul Baloche (*Open the Eyes of My Heart*)

Leader Scripture Exploration

- **Matthew 6:25-34** (Seek first the kingdom of God.)
- **Luke 11:11-13** (God cares for God's children.)
- **John 1:1-5** (In the beginning was the Word.)
- **John 3:16-21** (God loves God's children.)

 ## On Screen

Key points of presentation (PowerPoint® on CD)

Reminder Beads

Have the youth make beaded bracelets that remind youth of their relationship with God. Each colored bead has a special meaning and represents a specific aspect to our relationship with God. The colors represent the following:

- Black—sin and darkness
- Red—the blood of Jesus shed for the forgiveness of sins
- Blue—the water we are baptized with as an outward profession of belief and change
- White—the purity and cleansing received by grace
- Green—our growth in knowledge and faith as we mature in our walk
- Yellow/Gold—the rewards and riches awaiting us in heaven

 ## Focus Point

Video Option: *Bruce Almighty* (Start: 1:23:36—"You know what I do every night before I go to bed?"; stop: 1:29:20—"Get the backboard and brace.") (More information plus teaching points on CD)

Gaudy Greatness Option: Ahead of time, gather and also encourage youth to gather the tackiest, gaudiest, most ornate objects they can and bring them for this lesson. This activity should be fun, not costly nor mean toward anyone who might actually enjoy the objects. Point out that the word *gaud* refers to a showy ornament or trinket. How often in our lives do we treat God as "gaud"?

Focus Thoughts (Text and extension on CD)

Put all of your preconceived notions, your expectations, aside. Open your ears and listen with your heart. For some of you, this is the most important talk you'll need to hear. That's because the most important relationship you need in your life is one with God. God wants and needs you to be in relationship with God. And God wants and needs to be in a relationship with you.

Let's go back to the beginning—the very beginning. **John 1:1,** "In the beginning was the Word, and the Word was with God, and the Word was God." God is not a lone entity, but rather three in one (the Trinity)—Father, Son, and Holy Spirit. This idea is complex; even adults sometimes have trouble understanding and explaining it. How can God, Jesus, and the Holy Spirit be three separate entities and at the same time be one in the same? The important thing is that, either way, they are in relationship with one another. So God is, by definition, relational. From the beginning, God has been in relationship with the Son and the Holy Spirit.

Now, let's look also at the beginning of human life, Adam and Eve. God did not create one person, God created two people—to be in relationship with each other—and with God. Human beings are made in God's image; and if God is relational, then we must also be relational. We are meant to have relationships with others—especially with God.

Why is it so important to have a relationship with God? Well for one reason, God promises to support us and love us no matter what life throws our way. God also promises that a relationship where God is first, before all else, will result in all of our needs being provided for. (*Read aloud Matthew 6:31-33.*)

That doesn't mean that we get whatever we want or that life is easy once you have God as the center of your life. It does mean that we will always have what we need, including strength and support to get through the hard times.

Now, with sports, clubs, school activities, family commitments, and so on, it is easy to push God to the side. You are under a lot of pressure to succeed in the world so that you can get into a good school then find a good paying job so that you can buy a nice house and car and earn enough money to have nice things for your family. But the struggle that most of us get caught up in is that we're so busy trying to do all the right things to be successful by the world's standards that we lose sight of true success and forget to trust God. Our relationship with God ends up consisting of church on Sunday, youth group, and a prayer we say before meals. But God is God, not gaud—a mere trinket to be brought out on special occasions like a showy ornament.

We've looked at relationships with parents, friends, and boyfriends and girlfriends, and we've seen the importance of having healthy relationships in those areas. What would happen in your life if you made God first, if you had a relationship with God that resembled your very best relationship with your parents, or your very best relationship with your best friend, or your very best relationship with your boyfriend or girlfriend? God wants to be all of those things to you and more: parent, best friend, lover, and savior.

Remember how we talked about parents having a hard time letting go. Well God loves us so much that God is willing to let go and let us make our own choices. We call that "free will." We are not chess pieces being moved around a board, we are free to choose. Unfortunately, we've all made some poor choices; and we will again. But still, God's love comes through. God loves us so much, despite ourselves, that God gave Jesus, God's own son so that we would benefit (**John 3:16**).

God does not need "perfect" people who drive the right car, live in the right neighborhood, wear the right clothes, attend the right schools, eat in the nicest restaurants, or have the largest bank accounts. God loves people— people who make mistakes, people who want to be better people. God is interested in helping any and all of us by being in a close, personal relationship with us—a relationship that is honest and sincere, not token and superficial, like a trinket (like gaud on display).

Growing up is hard; imagine how hard it would be without the hope that God gives. Look at your relationship with God. What kind of shape is it in? Is it hurting? nonexistent? alive and active? I challenge you to take an honest look and make the necessary changes to have the relationship with God you need and that God offers—the relationship that leads to life abundant. Let's pray.

FOCUS GROUP (Questions and additional idea on CD)

- How would you rate your relationship with God on a scale of 1–10, with *1* being non-existent and *10* being better than you thought possible?
- What is a "good" relationship with God? What does it look like? How much time is spent with God, and what do you spend that time doing?
- What can you do to improve your relationship with God?
- What do you want from God in a relationship?
- What does God want from you in a relationship?

CLOSING

Prayers for Deeper Relationship With God

Pass around a bag of individually wrapped LifeSavers® candy or colored bits of paper. Have youth reach in and pull out one or two pieces. Have youth use the color of what they drew to pray for something specific related to their relationship with God. (Examples on CD)

Rita—A Demonstration

Using two ceramic masks and paint, you can create a powerful image for the youth about God making us new creations when we enter that relationship. (Instructions on CD)

Out and About

Drive somewhere in the youth van, or get parents to carpool the youth to a location for the meeting. The destination isn't as important as the journey. When you arrive, ask the youth how they reached their destination. Who was driving? Ask the youth who's in the driver's seat in their life—them or God? Do they trust God to get them to their destination?

Clown Communion

This is a very special way to end this series. (Instructions on CD)

Youth Witness Statement

Have a youth or two give a witness statement about his or her conversion and the difference God has made in his or her life. Have the youth tell what his or her life was like before and after God. The difference should be clear and easy to see. (How-to on CD)

UNDER CONSTRUCTION

BUILDING IT!

Building a relationship with God doesn't require a contractor's license or an architect's degree, but it does require work on our part. Having the right tools and blueprint will help youth construct a solid relationship with our Holy Savior. In truth, building that relationship strong is a lifelong process—we're always "under construction."

APPETIZERS

Publicity Ideas: *Invite more youth to the Christian journey. Select any or all of the ideas below. Combine or simplify.*

◉ Buy or find at a garage sale a set of Lincoln Logs or a similar building toy. Hang a tag from each piece with the theme, location, dates, and time listed. Then either mail them to each youth or hand them out at the door on Sunday mornings or at youth group the week before beginning this theme. Give out some extras for your youth to pass along to a friend.

◉ Make yard signs to advertise the theme all over the community. Have each member of your youth leadership team place one in his or her yard to generate curiosity and interest.

◉ Go to a local lumber yard or home improvement store and buy lots of carpenters' pencils. Wrap a sticker around each one, showing dates and times of the study. Hand them out on Sunday morning at church, or give them to your leadership team and ask them to hand out the pencils at school one day.

◉ On the Sunday closest to the start of the theme, place a youth wearing a carpenter's apron filled with brochures standing at each entrance to the church. Brochures should include information about where and when the theme will begin. Mail them to youth who may not be in worship. Use the theme logo to create a brochure or flyer. (Logo design on CD)

◉ Construct a little playhouse to sit in front of the church. (Be sure to get church leadership permission beforehand.) Hang a sign saying, "Under Construction," on each side and then list dates and times. (Note: After the theme is over, donate the playhouse to the children's ministry of your church.)

DRINKS

" 'Lord, when was it that we saw you ... thirsty and gave you something to drink? ...' 'Truly, I tell you, just as you did it to one of the least of these' " (Matthew 25:37, 40a).

Service project ideas

CㅇMBOS MEnU

Main Dishes

Weekly Program Options: *Choose one or all; do in any order. Check each description for variations and the fixin's. Invite a team of youth to decide how to personalize each program.*

1. **The Building Site**—Building anything requires a firm foundation, which takes preparation and the right materials. Unfortunately, it's often easier to do what's quickest, rather than what's best. Help your group construct a life-long relationship with God that has a solid foundation and a firm footing to withstand life's storms.

2. **Body Building**—People generally do not enjoy calisthenics, but they do them to keep their body physically strong. We are whole persons, and taking care of our physical body also reflects our care for our spiritual relationship with God. Lead the youth toward building bodies that are temples worthy of our king.

3. **Building Together**—It's not enough to work on our own relationship with God individually. Becoming a strong Christian requires a concerted effort to build others up as well. We do not live in a bubble; we are interdependent. Even Jesus prayed for his friends. Convince the youth that what we do matters to other people in a very big way.

4. **Build It Strong**—Being a Christian doesn't ensure us a trouble-free life. We're still going to have things that shake us up. Help each of the youth build a relationship with God through church attendance, prayer, and service that is like the Energizer Bunny™—it just keeps going and going.

Spice It Up

Theme Decorations: *Look at your space. Use your imagination. Enlist youth to help decorate.*

🎞 Gather old appliance boxes from a local store. Decorate each one to look like a building of some kind. Line the walls of the youth area or hallway with these buildings.

🎞 Using butcher paper, design a cityscape mural reflecting different kinds of buildings. Include at least one with the sign saying, "Under Construction." Hang the mural on one wall of the youth room. Consider creating a part of that mural to be a "graffiti" wall, where youth may sign in each week and write their favorite sayings, Bible verses, announcements, and prayers.

💿 Decorate the youth area like a construction site. Have a pile of dirt in one corner (be sure to put plastic underneath to protect the floor), a stack of lumber in another area, some concrete blocks sitting around, and other "scrap" items you might see on a work site. Gather some work tools and some water coolers. Hang a work belt on the wall, filled with screwdrivers, measuring tapes, hammers, and more. String up yellow caution tape. Then, as the youth arrive, hand out safety goggles or yellow hard hats to give the work site a real air of authenticity. (Link for inexpensive yellow hard hats on CD)

THE BUILDING SITE

Have It Your Way!

Choose from, adapt, or rearrange these elements to create the best soul feast for your youth group.

The Fixin's

More fun stuff to make the theme extra special! Your choice.

🔘 Munchies

- Praline Bricks
- Rock Bottom Chocolate Pie
- Rock Candy—Visit your local tourist attraction where they almost always sell rock candy in the gift shop. Buy enough for each person to have one or just buy a few, crack them, and let everyone taste a bunch of different flavors.
- Waffle Cookies—They look like bricks and mortar.
- Rocky road ice cream can be purchased in most grocery stores under several different brand names.

Popular Songs

Use these before and/or after the program to engage the youth. These are some options. Try to include the latest appropriate popular songs.

- "Rock On," by David Essex (*David Essex—His Greatest Hits*)
- "Rocky Mountain High," by John Denver (*Definitive All-Time Greatest Hits*)

Worship and Praise Music

- "The Church's One Foundation"
- "How Firm a Foundation"
- "Rock of Ages"
- "Jesus Is the Rock"

SOUL FOOD: Building a strong faith that will weather life's storms requires a firm foundation.

SCRIPTURE: Luke 6:46-49 (Building on rock versus building on shifting, unstable sandy ground)

Games

Lego® Race

Find out who the real builders in your group are with this fun Lego® game. Divide the group into smaller teams. Buy a small Lego® vehicle for each group. Put the pieces of each vehicle into a plastic bag. Do not give the youth anything that shows them that the completed item is a vehicle or how it will look.

Line up the teams just as in a relay race. On "go," the first person in each line runs to the table where the pieces are and has thirty seconds to work on putting the Lego® item together. At thirty seconds, time is called and the next person on each team tries. First team to complete the Lego® item is wins! Note: It is not necessary that the vehicle look exactly like the picture on the box, only that it look like a vehicle.

Walk This Way

Walking in circles was never this much fun before. Set up two wading pools across the room from each other. Have one filled with sand and one filled with gravel.

Play Follow the Leader around and through the two pools, doing silly things like hopping on one foot, "flying" with arms outstretched, skipping. Play "Walk This Way" in the background as you play around. Have a D.J. set up to stop the music at random intervals. When the music stops, the person(s) in each of the pools is out. Continue playing until only one person is left. That person is the winner. Award the winner a piece of rock candy.

🔘 Share and Care Groups (Text on CD)

Checking in: Highs and lows of the week, prayer requests, and prayer

Warm up: Many of us have ideas of what our future dream home would look like, but have you thought about where you would build it? Where would you choose to live if money were not an issue? What is more important to you—a great big house or a lot of land? Which would you choose—a luxurious house or a modest house? a site way out in the country or one in the middle of town? Why?

Focus Point

Video Options: *Jesus,* the Jesus Film Project video, which relates the Gospel of Luke. (Start: 00:22; stop: 00:25). Jesus explains the parable of the sower, another story in which he emphasizes the importance of having a strong basis on which to build your faith. (See *www.jesusfilm.org*.)

Activity Option: Build a Castle—Grab some wading pools, fill them with sand, and let the fun begin. Divide the youth into small groups to design and build the best sandcastles ever. After awarding a prize for the best design, turn big fans on the structures. Then dump water on them. Watch how the structures deteriorate. Discuss which (wind or water) created the biggest change.

Focus Thoughts (Text on CD)

It is easy for us to take buildings for granted. After all, they are everywhere; and for the most part, we can trust them to stand solid and not fall in on us. But let's think about what goes into creating a trustworthy building.

One of the most important considerations involves the site itself. Different types of structures have different requirements. Some structures can be built on the beach; but you are more likely to see a house on stilts there than a skyscraper, for example. Houses on a hillside, unless they are firmly anchored in bedrock, can easily become casualties of a mud slide. Insurance companies raise red flags when someone wants to build in a flood plain—no matter that it hasn't suffered a flood in 40 years—it could!

We want to build a relationship with God. To make it strong, we need the right foundation, or our "building," our relationship with God, will not last.

So, what *is* the right foundation for a strong relationship with God? Jesus tells us straight.

(*Read aloud* **Luke 6:46-49.**)

If we simply read the words and maybe even repeat them but do not use them as a guide for our lives, then our faith is like building a house on the sand. It will not last! It's easy to call Jesus, "Lord, Lord!" It's harder to do what he tells us. But living what Jesus teaches makes the difference between a faith that will collapse at the first sign of life's troubles or one that will weather the storms and see us safely through.

How then do we build a foundation that is rock solid? The building blocks lie in the Word of God. You have to first read the Bible to see what Jesus says to do. You can't begin to live Jesus' teachings if you don't know what they are.

Here are some ways you can learn from the Bible and know what Jesus is telling you about how to live:

• Participate in Sunday school.
• Participate in Bible study opportunities.
• Learn how to study the Scripture.
• Read your Bible at home.
• Use devotional books or magazines.

Make a commitment to build a strong foundation of faith. Life will send its storms; be ready! Let's pray.

Leader Scripture Exploration

• **Deuteronomy 6:1-9** (The Shema: Love God)
• **1 Chronicles 29:16** (Thanksgiving for the building materials)
• **Matthew 7:24-29** (The wise and the foolish builders)
• **1 Corinthians 3:5-16** (We build on Christ as our foundation.)

On Screen

Key points in Focus Thoughts (PowerPoint® on CD)

Out and About

• Go rock climbing. Visit a local gym with a rock-climbing wall for a great team-building experience. Many gyms will offer an introductory safety course and an hour or two of rock climbing for a special rate just to get you to try out this new and exciting sport. Better yet, find someone who can work with the group on rock climbing or rappelling at an outdoor site.

• Go on a Photo Scavenger Hunt. Divide the youth into groups of 4–5 (to fit in a car). Arrange to have transportation and an instant camera, digital camera, or videocamera for each group. (Some youth or leaders may have cameras with photo capability.) Give each group a list of locations to visit and a deadline; then turn them loose (with an adult chaperone, of course) to record their own group visiting as many of the locations as possible. When everyone returns view and enjoy reliving the adventures. (List on CD)

(Additional Idea on CD)

💿 Service Projects

• Create a rock garden. Many churches have an unused corner or two outside of the building that would make an ideal site for a beautiful rock garden. Visit a local garden center for advice on what plants would thrive for your location and climate.

• This building is for the birds. Buy enough birdhouse kits for individuals or small groups of youth to work on together. When the houses are completed, place them on posts around the church grounds or sell them as a fundraiser for a service project.

(Additional ideas on CD)

Art Projects

• Mezuzah: Have the youth make a *mezuzah*. A mezuzah is a case placed on the doorpost of a house in keeping with the commandment that God gave us in Deuteronomy 6:4-9—We are to keep God's words in our minds and our hearts and inscribe them on the doorposts of our houses. These cases are decorated on the outside and have a rolled up scroll containing the biblical reference on the inside. Anyone who enters the house is to touch the mezuzah as a sign of love for God and as a reminder of the words therein. (While Jewish Law requires specifics about the building of these cases, for your youth, a simple pouch or pocket or small matchbox would work fine.)

• Sand Art: Hand out cardstock, glue, and some colored sand and let each youth design a self-portrait. Hang the finished portraits in a prominent hallway of the church for everyone to see and enjoy.

FOCUS GROUP

One thing that is important in studying the Bible is to look at the context of the particular passage, which for today is Jesus teaching a great crowd and his disciples (Luke 6:17). (*Read aloud* **Luke 6:27-36 and 37-42.**) These teachings are what Jesus is referring to in today's passage as "what I tell you to do."

• What in these two passages surprised you? What had you not heard before? What new learning did you gain from reading these passages?
• How hard or easy do you find it to do what Jesus is telling you in these passages? Why? What helps? What makes it harder?
• Is it possible for us to be Christians without reading the Bible?

💿 CLOSING

Sand or Rock?

Have a plastic container of sand and another plastic container of rocks, some candles, and matches handy.

Light the candles and sit on the floor in a circle around them. Reread the Scripture, and then place the Bible in the middle of the circle next to the candles. Remind the youth that God is calling us to build on a strong foundation. Dip your hand into the plastic container of sand, lift some sand, and let the sand run through your fingers. After doing so, pass the sand container to the person on your left. Then pick up the container of rocks. Remind the youth that God doesn't just want lip-service from us. God wants our actions to live up to our beliefs. Take a rock out of the plastic container and pass the container to the person on your left. As you pass it, say these words to the person to your left, "Build your life on a solid foundation." Then pass the container of rocks to him or her. Each person, in turn, will take a rock and say the same.

After everyone has felt the sand and chosen a rock, close with the youth benediction (**Numbers 6:24-26**).

💿 An Invitation

Put together information about Bible study opportunities that are available in your church or area. Bring devotional books or magazines to show (and give) to youth. Create a sign-up sheet for youth to express interest in forming a Bible study. Close with prayer expressing a desire to know and do what Jesus is tell us. (Suggested resources on CD)

BODY BUILDING

SOUL FOOD: God has given us amazing bodies; keeping them healthy honors God and our relationship with God.

SCRIPTURE: 1 Corinthians 6:12, 19-20 (Your body is a temple of the Holy Spirit.)

GAMES

Muscle Power

Divide the youth into groups of 6–10 for this fun display of muscle power and ingenuity. Gather 2 six-foot-long boards and one large trash can per team. Each team's task is to get all of their team members to the other end of the room without stepping on the floor. Watch the fun and creativity as the groups try to win this wacky race.

Body Twistin'

Scrounge around in the game closets at church and home and dust off Twister® for some body-building fun!

SHARE AND CARE GROUPS (Text on CD)

Checking in: Highs and lows of the week, prayer requests, and prayer

Warm up: What is your best physical attribute? What is one thing that you would change about your body if you could? Rate your body on a scale of 1 to 10 with *1* being the lowest and *10* being the best. (Be careful on this question. Discuss it only if the group has already developed trust and confidence in one another.)

FOCUS POINT

Video Option: *Shrek 2* (2004) (Start:18:25; stop: 20:44) Fiona is crying because the visit home is not going well. The fairy godmother appears and sings about all the things she can do for Fiona to make things better for her. If time allows, discuss what it is each person would ask for from a fairy godmother.

Activity Option: Set up a continuum. Designate one side of the room, "I totally agree," and the opposite side, "I totally disagree." Draw an imaginary

Have It Your Way!

Choose from, adapt, or rearrange these elements to create the best soul feast for your youth group.

THE FIXIN'S

More fun stuff to make the theme extra special! Your choice.

Munchies

- Veggie tray with low-fat dip
- Have a fat-free or sugar-free snack buffet, allowing the youth to sample a wide range of good choices for snacking.
- Fruit basket

Popular Songs

Use these before and/or after the program to engage the youth. These are some options. Try to include the latest appropriate popular songs.

- "Who Am I?" by Casting Crowns (*Live From Atlanta*)
- "I'm Not Cool," by Scott Krippayne (*All of Me*)
- "All Fall Down," by MercyMe (*Almost There*)

Worship and Praise Music

- "Blessed Be the Name of the Lord"
- "From the Rising of the Sun"
- "He Knows My Name"
- "Enough"

Reminder

You may have youth who have physical disabilities or youth who are struggling with eating disorders. Be sensitive to their realities as you plan and present this Combo.

 Other Movie Options

Choose one of these, or ask students to recommend a more recent release. Be sure to preview your selection to avoid any content that would be objectionable in your setting. Remember that you must have a video license.
(Video licensing information on CD)

• *Shrek* (2001)
• *Shallow Hal* (2001)

Leader Scripture Exploration

• **Psalm 139:13-14** (How wonderfully we are made.)
• **Romans 12:1** (Present your bodies as a living sacrifice, holy and acceptable to God.)
• **1 Corinthians 3:9** (We are God's servants.)

On Screen

Key points in Focus Thoughts (PowerPoint® on CD)

Talk Tip

Change the talk about the effects of lack of sleep, over-eating, and too little exercise into a dialog with the group. Engage the youth with questions so that they think them through and come up with some of the results. List the answers for all to see on large sheets of paper or a markerboard.

Out and About

Visit a local science center, college or university, or hospital where someone can show—with models, charts, and other visual aids—just how intricate and amazing this "body by God" is.

---

line between the two points. Explain that the youth may place themselves at any point on the continuum, depending upon what they believe and to what degree. After each statement, invite a few youth to tell why they placed themselves where they did. (Questions on CD)

Focus Thoughts (Text on CD)

*(**Personalize your introductory remarks.**) Seeing a full-length picture of myself recently immediately spurred me into action. I got on the Internet and waded through a sea of information on dieting—from low-carb to low-fat to eating right for your own blood type. I spent days studying the information—all the while treating myself to my favorite goodies. None of the diets talked about the benefits of eating a whole row of Oreos® in one sitting, and I wanted to make sure I got my fill prior to starting the diet. I didn't want to feel deprived. When I finally chose a diet, I had gained an additional five pounds as a result of all the "getting ready."*

Isn't it ironic how we take care of ourselves? Or more to the point, isn't it amazing how we don't take care of ourselves? Even when we're not super-sizing our portions, we're dousing our foods in rich sauces and gravies that have dangerously high fat contents. Snacks consist of sweet snack cakes, cookies, candy, or whole bags of chips.

Many of us aren't involved in any kind of regular exercise. "Too busy," we say, when we really mean, "Not interested!" Too often we take escalators and elevators, instead of using the stairs; we drive or catch a ride to places when we could easily walk.

And while we feel the effects of sleep deprivation, we never really think about the loss of productivity or attention that it causes us. In fact, recent studies show that most teenagers suffer seriously from lack of sleep.

Why does any of this matter anyway? What does the Bible say about taking care of ourselves?

(*Read aloud **1 Corinthians 6:19-20.***)

What can it possibly mean to consider our bodies as temples? Why would God care about our bodies?

First of all, our bodies were intricately designed by the Creator.

(*Read aloud **Psalm 139:13-14.***)

Have you ever considered the workings of the human body? Have you thought about the interdependence of each body system? Each part is designed to work with the other parts in awesome and incredible ways. Abusing these parts and systems by overeating, under-exercising, and not resting creates a strain on our bodies that over time causes them to falter.

When we do not treat our bodies well, the side effects are multiplied. Lack of sleep affects the ability to concentrate, which affects our learning and education. Over-eating causes blood sugar levels to fluctuate erratically which, in turn, causes severe mood swings and difficulties in getting along with others. Infrequent exercise causes sore muscles. Too little exercise actually causes the muscles to waste away. Without regular, intentional exercise we lose the ability to sustain activity over time, not to mention simply being able to enjoy playing and having fun together.

In addition to these basics of the right food, regular exercise, and enough rest, we face the temptation of things that some people call "cool" but that actually are harmful to our bodies. Smoking, drinking, drug and substance abuse, and unprotected sex all play into the health of our own bodies, as well as the image we maintain of ourselves.

The bottom line is that not treating our bodies as temples causes them harm. Our whole being suffers—physically, emotionally, socially, and spiritually. Not treating our bodies as temples also sends the message to God that we don't value God's gift of this body. We disrespect rather than honor God.

We have a heavenly Father who has blessed us in so many ways, but we must do our part. In **Genesis 1:26-28,** we read that God put us in charge of the earth and told us to be good stewards of all there is. Do you think that God meant for us to take care of everything on earth—except ourselves? Aren't you worth at least as much in value to God as the birds of the air and the fish of the sea? God loves you.

So, how are you doing as a steward for God? How are you taking care of your temple? How are you honoring your relationship with God? Let's pray.

FOCUS GROUP (Questions on CD)

Read aloud **1 Corinthians 6:12-20.**
- What point is Jesus making in this passage?
- Why is so important to Jesus that we treat our bodies as temples?
- Why is our self-image so tied in with the way we look on the outside?
- How does knowing that God gave you your body as a gift to be treasured and valued make you feel?
- Where do you go from here?

CLOSING

Where Am I Now?

If your church has a gym or a fitness center, that is the perfect place for this closing. If not, consider contacting a local gym to use a fitness room there. Gather around the fitness equipment. Remind the youth that the Bible says that our bodies are temples; as such, we should respect and honor them by taking good care of them. And in respecting our bodies, we are honoring the Maker.

Close with an accountability circle. One youth who agrees to go first starts by finishing this sentence, "I know that my body is a temple, and I need to ask God's help with (*name some improvement that needs to take place*)." Each person, in turn, finishes that same statement. (*Allow persons to pass if they choose to.*)

Note: This activity requires much trust on the part of the youth. If your group is not ready to respect one another's feelings, simply ask each youth to pray silently for help from God. Then join together in the youth benediction (**Numbers 6:24-26**).

Feel God's Love (Litany on CD)

Close with a litany from **Psalm 139:1-18.** Pray with thanksgiving for the gift of being wonderfully created, known, and loved.

Support Groups

Consider ways to help your teens do better with their care for their health and physical well-being. (Ideas on CD)

Service Projects

- 30-Hour Famine: This is a good time for a lesson in appreciation at how really blessed most of us are as well as a chance to help others in their efforts to build stronger bodies as your group members experience a real fast. (Information on CD)

- Become justice advocates. Write the school administration and school board. Ask for access to more healthful choices for snacks and lunches. Ask for more opportunities for students to engage in physical exercise as well.

Poster

God Gives Us Free Will. What Decisions Will You Make? (Design on CD)

BUILDING TOGETHER

Have It Your Way!

Choose from, adapt, or rearrange these elements to create the best soul feast for your youth group.

The Fixin's

More fun stuff to make the theme extra special! Your choice.

🔘 Munchies

- Friendship Candy
- "Build It!" Night: Build your own sundae, baked potato, taco, or burger for a snack or meal. Have some parents help supply the fixin's.

Popular Songs

Use these before and/or after the program to engage the youth. These are some options. Try to include the latest appropriate popular songs.

- "Build Me Up, Buttercup," by The Foundations (*The Very Best of the Foundations*)
- "Easy to Be Hard," by Three Dog Night (*The Complete Hit Singles*)
- "Help Somebody," by Earth, Wind, and Fire (*Earth, Wind, and Fire*)
- "Bring Me to Life," by Evanescence (*Fallen*)
- "With a Little Help From My Friends," by the Beatles (*Sgt. Pepper's Lonely Hearts Club Band*)
- "Words," by the BeeGees (*Number Ones*)
- "I'll Be There," by Mariah Carey (*Greatest Hits*)
- "You Are So Beautiful," by Joe Cocker (*Ultimate Collection*)
- "You Raise Me Up," by Josh Groban (*Closer*)

Worship and Praise Music

- "What a Friend We Have in Jesus"
- "The Gathering"

SOUL FOOD: Building a relationship with God is not just about us; it requires building other people up as well.

SCRIPTURE: John 17:6-26 (Jesus prays for his friends.)

🔘 Games (Additional game on CD)

May I Help You?

Ahead of time, set up a buffet line with the supplies for hero sandwiches. Have each youth find a buddy to pair up with. With a bandanna or short piece of lightweight rope, tie the left hand of one youth to the right hand of his or her buddy. Line the youth up and instruct each pair to build a sandwich together using *only* their free hands. After going through the buffet line, each pair must sit down and eat the sandwich together. Note: If you want to make this a little harder, blindfold one member of each pair.

🔘 Group Effort (List of tasks on CD)

It requires everyone's assistance to be the winners in this game of teamwork and speed. Divide the youth into groups of about 10 and have them stand together in a separate area of the room. On "go," have each group complete a command given to them, using the members themselves. Each team scores a point for being the first group to complete the task. The team with the most points at the end of the game wins.

🔘 SHARE AND CARE GROUPS (Text on CD)

Checking in: Highs and lows of the week, prayer requests, and prayer

Warm up: What are the traits of a good friend? What characteristics do you look for in a friend? What is more important to you in a friend—honesty or trustworthiness? Do you prefer to have just one really close friend or is it more important to you to have a lot of friends? Do you hold grudges against people or do you forgive and forget?

FOCUS POINT

Video Option: *The Lion King* (1994) (00:08–00:09) The father explains to Simba how everything in the world is interdependent.

Activity Option: Divide into groups of five or six students. Give each group a plastic bag containing a small can of play dough and toothpicks. Be certain that each group has exactly the same amount of supplies with which to work. Then, instruct each group to build the highest structure possible in a ten-minute period. At the end of ten minutes evaluate each structure to see which group measured up! Then discuss the dynamics of the group. Talk about the characteristics of the people in each group: Who appeared to take a leadership role? Who was a contributor? Who was a good follower but didn't really come forward with ideas on how to build? Who was a good encourager (gave positive feedback to others)? How did each of those characteristics help the whole team?

FOCUS THOUGHTS (Text on CD)

Give an example of your own for this introduction: Recently my husband and I suffered through one of the hardest points in our lives when we buried his best friend. At a surprisingly young age, Gene was the victim of a massive heart attack while simply sitting at his desk one day.

When something like that happens, we become motivated to examine our priorities and to take stock of our own lives. So that's what I've been doing for the last few months. I've made some important discoveries about myself.

Give one or two examples of your own, such as these: Number one: I am a wife and mother, who is crazy in love with her husband and family but who doesn't always let them know that. I am often so busy and preoccupied with church "stuff" that my family has to take a back seat. I need to fix that. Number two: I am a sinner who keeps trying to do better but doesn't always succeed. There are so many mistakes I have made over and over; when will I ever learn? Thankfully, I rest in the knowledge that God continues to love me.

The other thing I found out about myself, though, is that I am a horrible friend. I really am. I take my friends for granted, don't always listen to them when they are pouring out their troubles, and rarely spend time to just be with them. I need to make some changes; I am not living what I believe.

The truth is that we need other people. We are not meant to live alone. When God created the earth, God designed us with the need to be with other people. No person can succeed in a healthy way without the interaction and contact of other people. Sometimes we think that we are solely responsible for ourselves or for saving the world. We don't need anyone else; we don't want anyone else. Other people just get in the way. But even the Lone Ranger had Tonto!

One of the most important lessons Jesus modeled for us was the necessity to develop and maintain close relationships with other people. He demonstrated the need to lift others up and support them in their difficulties. Remember the story of how Jesus healed Simon's mother-in-law? And what about the time he raised his friend Lazarus from the dead? We surely can't forget how he fed the thousands with a simple basket of fish and bread either. Whatever the circumstance, Jesus showed great compassion and support for the people. He was never too busy or too important to take time for others.

When Jesus knew that his time on earth was nearing an end, he prayed first for his friends. Many of us are familiar with the fact that Jesus prayed in the

Other Movie Options

Choose one of these, or ask students to recommend a more recent release. Be sure to preview your selection to avoid any content that would be objectionable in your setting. Remember that you must have a video license. (Video licensing information on CD)

- *Elf* (2003) (00:08–00:10) Buddy's dad explains the drawbacks of being a human in an elf's world.
- *Homeward Bound* (1993) (00:36–00:37) The scene shows Shadow and Chance commiserating with each other, thinking that Sassy had drowned because they weren't able to save her.

Leader Scripture Exploration

- **2 Corinthians 13:10** (Paul reminds the people that his authority, given by God, is for building up, not for tearing down.)
- **Ephesians 2:11-21** (In Christ, we are built together spiritually as a dwelling place for God.)
- **Ephesians 4:25–5:2** (Christ's new rules for life include building up one another.)

On Screen

Key points in Focus Thoughts (PowerPoint® on CD)

Building Up Others

Check out these great ideas for strengthening families, ministries within your church, and relationships between generations. (Ideas on CD)

⊙ Service Projects

Target a different group of church members to build up each week during the theme. Then find a way to appreciate that particular group. Suggestions might include:

- Muffins for Moms: Get together to make muffins. Set up a reception table for moms to come have coffee and muffins prior to church one Sunday morning. (Moms include any woman who has acted in the capacity of a mother, including grandmothers, aunts, adoptive mothers, guardians.)
- Doughnuts for Dads: This is the same idea as Muffins for Moms but is for persons acting as fathers. (Additional ideas on CD)

Blueprints

Contact a local architecture firm for some old blueprints that you can borrow for a display. After looking at the rooms that are included on a blueprint, challenge the youth to design a blueprint that illustrates who the friends in their lives are. (Example and Handout on CD)

Reminder Token

Provide supplies for the youth to make a bracelet, ankle bracelet, necklace, or key chain using beads that spell out *joy*.

Garden of Gethsemane for himself as he faced crucifixion. But before that, he prayed for his friends. We can do the same. We can learn from Jesus' example and start lifting one another up in prayer. When we pray for our friends, we are also building our relationship with God. And we will become a better friend because we are seeing the needs of our friends—not just our own. Here's a simple reminder: Make JOY your priority—Jesus first, Others second, and Yourself last. When you live in JOY, you will bless others and be blessed yourself. Let's pray.

⊙ Focus Group (Additional questions on CD)

- Jesus showed us what it means to lift other people up in prayer. (*Read John 17:6-26.*)
- What does Jesus mean when he says, "so they can be of one heart and mind as we are one heart and mind"?
- How important do you think it was for Jesus to pray for his followers?
- How important is it that we pray for our friends and families?
- In what other ways can we lift up our friends? Give some specific examples.
- Is it possible to support our friends even when they are doing things we know are wrong? How can we still love them as God loves us?

CLOSING

Prayers for Friends

Invite the youth to a time of prayer for their friends. Have them spend time at the altar and leave when they finish. Or have them pray with a partner or in small groups. Encourage them to pray aloud with each other. Yet another way is to have them write the name of a person on a piece of paper and leave it at the cross on the altar table.

A Strange Herd

Show the video clip from the movie *Ice Age* (2002), (00:52–00:55) that demonstrates our dependence on one another. End the clip with the statement, "We really are a strange herd." Remind the youth that while we all have idiosyncrasies and characteristics that sometimes make us difficult to get along with, we really are a part of a big family—God's family. As such, that makes us all members of the same "herd."

Ask, "How do you measure up as a member of the herd? Do you support it, or do you dig in your heels and hinder it? God calls us to help one another in the best ways we can. That means working hard to be a supportive member of the family." Circle up for the youth benediction (**Numbers 6:24-26**).

Jesus' Prayer (John 17:1b, 6-26)

In advance, recruit a youth or an adult with good dramatic or reading skills. Dress him or her in biblical garb. Dim the lights; create a scene that gives the illusion of simply overhearing Jesus in prayer. A good reader or speaker (exact words are not essential) can bring this powerful passage to life for the youth. End with silence, allowing the youth to leave as they are ready.

BUilD it StRoNG

SoUl FooD: Building a strong relationship with God doesn't require magic; however, it does require practice—Christian practices.

SCRiPTURe: Ephesians 6:10-18 (Paul gives advice to the people of Ephesus on staying strong.)

GaMeS

Incredible Hulk

See who has the most strength and endurance in this "stupid human trick." Ask for several volunteers. Give them each some hand weights (or have them take turns, and time each one). Ask the volunteers to stand with the weights held up over their heads for as long as they can. Have the rest of the group cheer them on as they compete for the Incredible Hulk Award. (Go to a garage sale or thrift shop ahead of time to pick up an inexpensive used trophy to give to the winner as the prize.)

Strongfoot

Place lots of marbles in the bottom of a small wading pool and then fill the pool with ice. Divide the youth into equal teams lined up at equal distances from the pool, and place a bucket in front of each line. On "go," the first person from each team runs to the pool; digs out a marble, using his or her toes; hobbles back to the line; and drops the marble into his or her team's bucket. Play continues with the next person in line repeating the steps until one team has 10 marbles in its bucket. No hands or other body parts are allowed for this chilly game.

SHaRe anD CaRe GRoUPS (Text on CD)

Checking in: Highs and lows of the week, prayer requests, and prayer

Warm up: Who is the strongest person you know? What kinds of things do you think that person does to stay strong? Who is the strongest person of faith you know? What tells you that he or she is strong? What kinds of things do you think that person does to stay strong spiritually?

Have It YoUR Way!

Choose from, adapt, or rearrange these elements to create the best soul feast for your youth group.

THe FiXiN'S

More fun stuff to make the theme extra special! Your choice.

Munchies

- Solid gold candy—Find those little baggies of gold nugget bubble gum, one per youth.
- Hard candy—Christmas is the best time to buy a huge assortment. Fill small Dixie cups (one per youth) with a variety.
- Have a tasting party to check out foods that come in soft and hard varieties, such as fried chicken (original and extra crispy), pizza (soft and crispy crusts), dinner rolls (soft and hard), cookies (Chips Ahoy and Chewy Chips Ahoy), and so forth. You get the picture!

Popular Songs

Use these before and/or after the program to engage the youth. These are some options. Try to include the latest appropriate popular songs.

- "I Will Survive," by Gloria Gaynor (*I Will Survive: The Anthology*)
- "Testify to Love," by Avalon (*Testify to Love: The Very Best of Avalon*)
- "Strong Tower," by Newsboys (*Devotion*)

Worship and Praise Music

- "Thy Word"
- "Be Bold, Be Strong"
- "The Word"

Leader Scripture Exploration

- **Romans 8:31-39** (Through Christ we are more than conquerors.)
- **Ephesians 2:19-22** (Jesus Christ is the cornerstone of our foundation in faith))
- **Colossians 1:3-14** (May you be made strong.)

 ## On Screen

Key points in Focus Thoughts (PowerPoint® on CD)

Out and About

Frequently when a church is built, a it has a cornerstone with the date engraved into it. Does your church have one? If so, take the students to check it out. Make sure to include the cornerstone idea (Ephesians 2:19-22) into any builds your group may undertake—whether it be a small project or a Habitat build!

Service Projects

- Contact Habitat for Humanity to schedule a youth build for your community. This takes much preparation, money, and manpower but is well worth the effort. (Information on CD)

- Meet with the your church's property management committee or trustees to find out what building projects are being planned for the future. Offer to help with any (or all) of these. Or make plans for the youth to do one of your own design, such as the following:

- building a playground or playground structure for the preschoolers
- building a cross for the sanctuary
- building a shed for storage
- painting a Sunday school room
- building shelves for a classroom

You're only limited by your own imagination. Not only will you do something great for the church, you'll build up the relationship between the young people in your church and the rest of the congregation!

 # Focus Point

Newscast Option: In advance, have a team of youth prepare to present a newscast—either live or videotaped and shown on a TV monitor for "authenticity." The news should be about a building collapse or a reporting of the story used at the beginning of the Focus Thoughts. (Information on CD)

(Additional activity on CD)

Focus Thoughts (Text on CD)

A local man hired a home builder to build a house. The man told the builder, "Build it the way you would like it." He was leaving it up the builder to decide the its design and building materials.

The home builder, left to his own devices, decided to build the house quickly, thinking that would please the soon-to-be homeowner. He also decided that, with no one to look over his shoulder and dictate the use of expensive materials, he would cut corners and use cheaper supplies.

Within a couple of months, the home was ready to move into, albeit small and cheaply built. When the builder handed over the keys, the new homeowner said, "Thank you so much for building this house; but you see, it wasn't ever intended for me. I noticed you around town, always building houses for other people. You appeared to do a good job, always completing a beautiful design and using high-quality materials. So I actually was having this house built for you. I hope you enjoy your own work!"

Isn't that the way things go for us sometimes? We take the easy route, the way with the least amount of effort; and then we wonder why we end up with a second-class result? We do that with our homework; with our chores; and unfortunately, with our relationships, including our relationship with God. We put in the least amount of effort and then wonder why things fall apart.

Other activities in our lives claim more attention and effort. We practice over and over many of the activities in which we participate. We go to the driving range to practice our golf swing, to the batting cages to practice our hitting, to the tennis courts to practice our returns, and to the gym to practice our free throws. When our coaches tell us to be there, we go.

And yet, what do we do to stay strong in our faith? How do we practice being a Christian? Could it be that we are so comfortable in our faith that we ignore its importance? Or for some of us, is it that we don't see the immediate returns; so we're not willing to put in more effort? Or could it be that for some of us, it's simply not that important.

Becoming a strong Christian is not something that just happens. It's not a magic potion or a matter of luck. It's the result of consistent choices to participate in the things that will bring us closer to God, such as prayer, Bible study, worship, service, and fellowship with other Christians. In other words, being a part of the body of Christ, the church.

In **Acts 2:46-47,** we are reminded that the people "followed a daily discipline of worship in the Temple followed by meals at home, every meal a celebration, exuberant and joyful, as they praised God. People in general liked what they saw. Every day their number grew as God added those who were saved" (*The Message*). Did you get that? They ate together and worshiped together; and as a result, they became stronger and more people were led to God.

In this world Christians face numerous temptations and forces that work for evil. We need to be strong spiritually. We don't get that way by taking shortcuts with our faith. Worshiping together, Christian fellowship, Holy Communion, prayer, Bible study, and service are among the practices of the faith that will build in us a strong faith. Our spiritual muscles are stronger when we do our exercises. With a strong relationship with God, we will be better able to overcome temptation and stand up against evil. Let's pray.

F⚬CUS GR⚬UP (Additional questions on CD)

Read aloud **Ephesians 6:10-18**. Read from more than one version; if possible, include *The Message*.

- Where do you see evil in the world? What kinds of temptations do people, including Christian youth face?
- What kinds of things do you find yourself battling spiritually?
- How easy or hard is it for you to stand up against evil or temptation?
- What are some of the "weapons" or helps God has given you? (Look specifically at the text.) What are other helps not named here?
- What do you think God is calling you to do about the evil in your own community or the temptations in your life?
- What does it mean when Paul says that God's Word is an indispensable weapon? How does knowing God's Word help you?

CL⚬SING

Build an Altar

Build a temporary altar, using concrete blocks or bricks; or have the youth each bring a rock with which to build an altar. Remind the youth that just as buildings are constructed to withstand the weather and natural disasters, a strong relationship with God ensures that we will be able to cope with life's ups and downs. Circle up for youth benediction (**Numbers 6:24-26**).

The Whole Armor

In this world we will encounter "spiritual forces of evil." But God does not leave us defenseless. God offers a complete set of armor (**Ephesians 6:10-18**). It is up to us to put on the whole armor of God—not just a piece here and there.

Bring out signs with these phrases on them as you talk through the Scripture: Belt of truth, breastplate of righteousness, gospel of peace, shield of faith, helmet of salvation, sword of the Spirit (the Word of God). Lay each on the altar, and invite the youth to claim *all* that God offers.

Youth Witness Statement

Invite a youth to talk about going through hard times or temptations and how his or her faith was sustaining. Ask him or her to also talk about what Christian practices help him or her be strong. (How-to on CD)

Re-issue the Invitation

Put together information about Bible study, service, and worship opportunities that are available in your church or area. Bring devotional books or magazines to show (and give) to youth. Create a sign-up sheet for youth to express interest in forming a Bible study. (Suggested resources on CD)

Worship Token

Drill a hole in the head of the kind of nails used for cement work. Give each student one to put on his or her keychain as a reminder to "build it strong."

Poster

Your Life Is Under Construction. Do You Have the Right Tools? (Design on CD)

GOOD BOOK LOOK

THE BIG PICTURE

The Bible is the basic resource of our faith. Maybe we know many of the stories and characters, or maybe we don't. We may be able to quote lots of verses, or maybe we can't. But do we really know the big picture of the Bible: How the Bible came to us, what the basic story of the Old and New Testaments is, and why the Bible is the basic resource of our faith? Use these four programs to give youth a good look at the Good Book and whet their appetite for more.

APPETIZERS (Additional ideas on CD)

Publicity Ideas: *Starting this theme is a great time to promote what your group is doing. These topic will attract some youth with big questions. Make sure that you have an open heart and mind. Show respect toward others, and allow the facts and God to do the rest.*

Send out teasers to grab attention and generate interest. Use the theme logo plus a catchy statement to create posters, cards, flyers, or an announcement on the church's Web page. Be sure to include the date, time, and location. (Suggestions on CD)

• E-mail the youth with the information; encourage them to forward the e-mail to their friends, with an invitation to come with them.

Make a large Wheel of Fortune and place it where it will be seen as youth go in and out of church. (Instructions on CD)

• Invite a team of youth to dramatize one or more Bible stories and to make a videotape of it. Make copies and send or give them to the youth to give to a friend, along with a personal invitation to come with them.

• Check out the older children's Sunday school class stash of past curriculum pictures. If it's OK with the teacher, take the pictures that show scenes from various Bible stories; and post the pictures in the hallways. Make a big sign saying: "Do you know these people? See you at the Good Book Look!"

DRINKS

" 'Lord, when was it that we saw you ... thirsty and gave you something to drink? ... ' 'Truly, I tell you, just as you did it to one of the least of these' " (Matthew 25:37, 40a).

Service project ideas

COMBO MENU

 ## Main Dishes

Weekly Program Options: *Choose one or all; do in any order. Check each description for variations and the fixin's.*

1. **How We Got the Word**—How did we get the Bible? Did it just drop out of heaven in the form we have it now, or is it more complicated than that? This program gives the story of how the Bible came to be and how it came to have authority in our lives.

2. **The B.C. Sprint**—We know some of the characters and stories. We may even be able to quote verses. But do we know the big picture of the Old Testament so that we can fit the details in to an overall framework? This program will give your group a sweeping overview of the Old Testament, with a focus on its major story line.

3. **Good News!**—The stories in the Gospels are probably the most familiar to youth, but putting the story of Jesus all together gives a very compelling picture of why we call Jesus "Lord."

4. **The Rest of the Story—and Me**—The rest of the New Testament is the story of the church: its birth at Pentecost, its phenomenal spread throughout the known world, the controversies it has struggled through, the hope it claims. Along the way, we find ourselves in the story too.

Spice It Up (Additional ideas on CD)

Theme Decorations: *Look at your space. Use your imagination. Give away or auction off purchased decorations as prizes at the end of the week or the theme.*

- Create a wall of favorite Bible verses or quotations about the Bible. Have members of your group and church leaders contribute. Write the verses, along with the persons' names, on large sheets of paper and post them on the wall. As starters, see the Old Testament Words of Life, Gospel Words of Life, and New Testament Words of Life handouts.

- Post Bible maps in an area; include contemporary pictures of biblical locations. One source is *Bible Student's Map Book* (Ordering Info on CD). These maps may be photocopied and enlarged and then colored in by the youth.

- If persons in your congregation have traveled to the Holy Land, invite them to display artifacts or show their photographs and tell about them as the youth gather.

- Consider giving everyone a new Bible. Prices start at under $5.00. See page 81. (Ordering information on CD)

(Additional Ideas on CD)

HOW WE GOT THE WORD

Have It Your Way!

Choose from, adapt, or rearrange these elements to create the best soul feast for your youth group.

The Fixin's

More fun stuff to make the theme extra special! Your choice.

Munchies

- Make a sheet cake with books of the Bible written on it.
- Have 66 cupcakes with the names of books written on them.

Worship and Praise Music

- "Blessed Be Your Name," by Passion (*Sacred Revolution*)
- "I Want to Know You (in the Secret)," by SonicFlood
- "Open the Eyes of My Heart, Lord," by SonicFlood (*Worship Together: I Could Sing of Your Love Forever*)
- "Amazing Love," by Mississippi Mass Choir (*Amazing Love*)
- "Awesome God," by Rich Mullins (*Winds of Heaven*)
- "El Shaddai"
- "Here I Am, Lord"
- "Thy Word Is a Lamp Unto My Feet"

Other Movie Options

Choose one of these other movies, or ask students to recommend a more recent release. Be sure to preview your selection to avoid any content that would be objectionable in your setting. Remember that you must have a video license.
(Video licensing information on CD)

- *The Greatest Story Ever Told* (1965)
- *Jesus of Nazareth* (1977)

SOUL FOOD:

For thousands of years people have recognized the Bible as the Word of God, but it did not just drop out of the sky one day. How we got the Word is an amazing story in itself.

SCRIPTURE: 2 Timothy 3:14-17 (All Scripture is inspired by God and profitable.)

Games

Famous Couples of the Bible (Examples on CD)

Create individual sheets with names of as many of the "famous couples" as you need for your group; include the Scripture references. Tape one sign on the back of each person. Tell the group that their challenge is to try to find out who they are and who their partner is. They can go up to other members and have others look at their back. Then they can ask yes or no questions. They cannot ask the person to tell them what name is. They can ask, for example: Is it a male? Is this person in the Old Testament? Does this person have a book named after them? (Debriefing questions on CD)

Bible Scavenger Hunt (Examples on CD)

Depending on your group size, form two or more teams and position them around the walls of the room with yourself in the middle. Give each team a Bible. Tell the teams that this is a scavenger hunt. You are going to call out something that is in the Bible—a character, an event, a story, a verse. Each team is to try to find the reference where the item is found. When a team finds it, they are to run to the center (bringing the Bible) and show you where the item is. The first team gets *X* points, the second team gets *Y* points, and so forth.

SHARE AND CARE GROUPS

Checking in: Highs and lows of the week, prayer requests, and prayer

Warm up: Hold up a Bible. Tell the group that you are going to pass the Bible around the circle to each person. When individuals receive it, they are to hold it for a few moments and then tell about their reactions to the Bible: their thoughts, their feelings about the Bible, what they wonder, any memories associated with the Bible—in short, whatever it evokes as they hold it. Tell them that there are no right or wrong answers.

 Focus Point

Headline News—The Bible is both a source of unity and of controversy among Christians. Controversy stems from basically two sources: 1) How people approach the Bible—as literal truth or as inspired revelation of God; and 2) how they interpret the Bible, which is not always easy. The Bible continues to make headline news even today. (Activity on CD)

Which One Is the Bible?—Some youth may need an introduction to translations and versions. (Activity on CD)

Focus Thoughts (Interactive text on CD)

Where there are blanks in the text, use those as opportunities for youth to give answers. Some of the answers are on the PowerPoint® presentation. Be sure to preview it and practice your timing.

Anyone who has ever been around the church knows that the Bible is important to Christians. But lots of us only know bits and pieces about what's in the Bible, how it came to be, and what makes it so important. Today, we're going to begin putting those pieces together so we get the big picture of the Bible. I'll need you to help me fill in the blanks from time to time with what you already know.

When you look at this book, you may be surprised to know that the Bible is not really one book, but ___ (66) books. It was written more than ___ (1600) years. It took 1500 of those years to put together the Old Testament and 100 to do the New Testament. More than ___ (40) people had a hand in writing the Bible; some of those were kings, prophets, leaders, and people who knew Jesus. The original documents were written in ___ (3) languages: Hebrew, Greek, and Aramaic. Today you can find translations of at least portions of the Bible in more than ___ (2,000) languages!

The Bible is the most influential book in the world. These specific words, about specific people, in specific cultures, at specific times long ago have become God's Word for all people in all cultures and all times. These Scriptures began changing people's lives for the better nearly _____ (3,500) years ago; they continue to do so today.

The Bible has ___ (2) main parts: _____ (Old Testament) with 39 books and _____ (New Testament) with 27. You may be surprised to know that in some versions of the Bible there is a third part, called the Apocrypha, which means "hidden books." These books may or may not be in the Bible you have, but they would certainly be in the Bibles used by Catholic and Orthodox Christians. Protestants count these books as informative, but not as a basis for belief.

The Hebrew Bible, what we also call the Old Testament, didn't start out as a book, but as stories told and retold. Imagine people sitting around a campfire and telling the stories of the Creation or Abraham and Joseph and Moses. That's what we call "oral tradition." These stories were passed down from generation to generation long before they were ever written down. Oral tradition is one reason why sometimes there are more than one version of the same story. And that's OK. The Bible doesn't have to have all the facts exactly right in order to show us truth! Other parts of the Hebrew Bible were

Create-a-Video

In advance, have a team of youth pick a favorite Bible story, create a skit based on it, then film the skit. Use it for publicity or for the Focus Point.

Background Info

Check your Bible; many editions will include a preface or articles that can be very informative.

Leader Scripture Exploration

- **Nehemiah 8:1-8** (Our understanding and worship of God is based on the Bible.)
- **Luke 1:1-4** (The Bible contains the truth concerning the things we have been taught.)
- **John 20:30-31** (These signs have been written that we might believe and have life.)
- **Hebrews 1:1-4** (God has spoken to us in many and various ways.)

On Screen

Key points in Focus Thoughts (PowerPoint® on CD)

Talk Tip

Give each youth a Bible during the talk; encourage them to refer to it. Make this talk interactive. Some youth may already know portions of this information; you may affirm their knowledge. Be sure not to make too big a deal about filling in the blanks, however, since for some youth, this information will be brand new. Use the information to set the context for inviting youth into deeper knowledge of these life-giving Scriptures.

Out and About

Visit a church in another denomination to see what role the Scripture plays in their worship and life. Ask the youth to note how this is similar to and different from their own church.

If there is college or university nearby, or a seminary, see whether they have a display of Bibles and religious manuscripts. If they do, arrange a visit to see some of these documents, and have someone do a presentation on the Bible. Some churches an synagogues also have collections of Bibles and manuscripts in their libraries.

 Service Projects

Volunteer to assist <u>Gideons International</u> in distributing Bibles in the area. (<u>Link on CD</u>)

Do a Bible drive to get Bibles to give to other churches, shelters, community centers, groups that work in impoverished areas. Don't forget that the Bibles can be in the appropriate language (for example, Spanish). (<u>Link to website for donations</u>)

 Poster (<u>Design on CD</u>)

The Bible Tells Us Who We Are and Whose We Are.

Youth Witness Statement

- Throughout this series, invite various youth to talk about their experience in a Bible study or in reading the Bible.
- Have individual youth quote their favorite Bible passage or tell about their favorite Bible story or person and talk about what it means to them.

Announcements

Be sure to publicize other opportunities for Bible study, such as <u>3V Bible Studies</u>, <u>Synago</u> Groups, <u>Youth DISCIPLE</u>, and (not-to-be-overlooked) Sunday school. (<u>Ordering info on CD</u>)

written down from the beginning. Some of those were stories or sayings; others were psalms and prayers used in worship.

The Temple in Jerusalem was the most important place for Jews to worship and to make their sacrifices to God, but at one point in their history the people were conquered. Many were carried off to Babylon in what we call "The Exile." Psalm 137 is very poignant: "How could we sing the Lord's song in a strange land?" In other words, how do we worship God without the Temple, a priesthood, and the practices of sacrifice? The answer was a new way to worship—through the reading and interpretation of Scriptures. Over time there was a need to "set the canon," in other words, to agree upon what would be the official Scriptures among all the stories and writings. That was completed by the Jews in 90 A.D. The list they set way back then is the same for us today.

The Old Testament includes four major parts: _____, _____, _____. (the Law/Torah, History, the Writings, and the Prophets). These are the Scriptures that Jesus knew and quoted! They continue to have meaning for us today.

Like the Old Testament, the stories that are in our New Testament about Jesus were at first just told person to person. People couldn't keep the good news to themselves! The more people told the stories of Jesus, the more churches formed. The first written portions of the Bible were the letters sent from Paul to the various churches: Corinth, Galatia, Philippi and so on—you probably recognize those names! The Gospels came later.

The New Testament includes four_____ (Gospels), a book of history _____ (Acts), twenty-one letters by _____ (Paul) and others, and the Book of Revelation, which gives hope to all Christians because it is the story of God's ultimate triumph.

What's so important about the Bible? The Bible is a window through which we see, understand, and grow to love God more and more, and it's a guidebook through which we learn how to live as God's people.

(*Read aloud **2 Timothy 3:16-17**.*)

Through the Scriptures we learn who we are and Whose we are. The more we become a "people of the Book," the more our lives and the lives of others are changed—for the better! Let's pray.

FoCUS GRoUP (<u>Additional questions on CD</u>)

- What parts of the presentation were you already familiar with?
- What parts surprised you? What did you learn?
- What new questions do you have?
- What do you think about the idea that the Bible has a history and that it has developed over time?

CLoSiNG

Bible Challenge

Hold up a Bible. Remind the youth that this book is a window to God and a book that can guide them to the joy of life. Challenge them to 1) read their Bibles this week, 2) to look for Scripture that has special meaning for them, and 3) to bring their Bible with them next week. Sing "Thy Word" to close.

THE B.C. SPRint

SOUL FOOD: The Old Testament is the story of the relationship between God and God's people, the Jews. It unfolds over nearly 2000 years and is told in the 39 books of the Hebrew Bible, but it is one consistent story.

SCRIPTURE: Psalm 108:3-4 (Praise for God's steadfast love and faithfulness)

 Games

Old Testament Wheel of Fortune

Create the wheel out of poster board. You can use either dollar amounts or point amounts. You can use blackboards, markerboards, or newsprint for the secret phrase and block each letter with a 8-by-11 sheet of paper taped over it. Then play the game just like the TV version. Use phrases from the Old Testament. (Examples and rules on CD)

Speed Verses

Use these familiar Old Testament statements, and have teams compete to answer first. Give each team (up to four teams) a bell or buzzer. Allow the team members to consult. If the first to buzz in does not answer correctly, give the other teams a chance. Give prizes for the winners. (Game questions on CD)

Share and Care Groups

Checking in: Highs and lows of the week, prayer requests, and prayer

Warm up: In the game, which answers were familiar or easy? Which were new or difficult?
(Additional questions on CD)

Focus Point

Video Option: Show a brief clip from *The Ten Commandments*. You may want to pick one of the more dramatic scenes (Moses being cast into the river, Moses at the burning bush with God speaking, Moses and the children of Israel crossing the sea) to grab the group's interest in the stories of the Old Testament.

Have it YOUR WAY!

Choose from, adapt, or rearrange these elements to create the best soul feast for your youth group.

THE FIXIN'S

More fun stuff to make the theme extra special! Your choice.

Munchies

- Fruit and Nut Bites
- Unleavened Bread
- Lentils and Rice
- Offer some traditional Middle Eastern foods, such as olives, dates, figs, almonds, pistachios, humus, pita bread and dip.
- Praise and reward youth who brought a Bible with them. Give them a "sweet treat, " such as a Kudos® candy bar. Keep encouraging others to bring Bibles for the next two weeks.

Worship and Praise Music

- "Blessed Be Your Name," by Matt Redman (*Worship Together: Here I Am to Worship 2*)
- "God of Wonder," by The Marantha! Singers (*Praise 17: In Your Presence*)
- "Ancient of Days" (*16 Biggest Praise and Worship Songs*)

Other Movie Options

Choose one of these other movies, or ask students to recommend a more recent release. Be sure to preview your selection to avoid any content that would be objectionable in your setting. Remember that you must have a video license.
(Video licensing information on CD)

• *The Bible: In the Beginning* (1966)

Create-a-Video

Have teams of volunteers pick a favorite Old Testament story, create a skit based on the story, then film the skit.

On-the-Street Interviews

Humorous on the street interviews, asking people who they think some of the lesser known Old Testament characters are. Who was Nahum? Na-who? OK, how about Zephaniah? Bless you!

Leader Scripture Exploration

• **Deuteronomy 24:17-22** (God commands caring for the helpless.)
• **Psalm 78** (God's goodness and Israel's ingratitude)
• **Psalm 138** (God's steadfast love)

On Screen

Key points in Focus Thoughts
(PowerPoint® on CD)

Prop Option: Have a Hebrew Bible for the group to look at. Your pastor may have one of these or you may be able to get one from the local library. If not, so a search on the internet for "Hebrew manuscript" under images. Print one for the group to look at.

Speaker Option: Have someone with a Jewish background talk to the group about the importance of the Scriptures in Judaism.

FOCUS THOUGHTS (Text on CD)

Today we're doing the "B.C. Sprint" through the Old Testament! You know what *B.C.* stands for. (*Ask the youth.*) *Before Christ*—that's a lot of years to cover. So we'll be racing through them, just touching some high points; but I want you to have a sense of the big picture. The Old Testament, the Hebrew Bible, is filled with all kinds of stories and other writings that tell one grand story about God and humans. Let's get started.

(*Show the PowerPoint® presentation The B.C. Sprint. Intersperse your own comments and additional information to help make this overview come alive for the youth. Let your love for the Scriptures come through.*)

After that sprint, take a breath; and let's talk about the big-picture story:

The Old Testament shows us God at work in human history. We discover an amazing God, worthy of our worship. We discover that God chooses to be in relationship with us! That's amazing in itself! We discover that God cares for all people! God is faithful. (*Read aloud **Psalm 108:3-4**.*)

The Old Testament also shows us ourselves. We discover how easy it is to turn away from this loving God, to do what we want, to focus on only ourselves. We also discover that life outside of a relationship with God only adds to the brokenness and injustice that mess up the perfection of what God desires for us and for all!

The Old Testament shows us God, who despite our human failings, continues to love us, to deliver us, and to give us second chances. We call that "grace." God continues to invite us into a loving relationship, to work with God toward wholeness, justice, and love for all!

That's the real story in the Old Testament. Let's pray.

FOCUS GROUPS (Additional questions on CD)

• What got your attention or stood out in the presentation?
• Why is the Old Testament important?
• If we did not have the Old Testament, what would we lose?
• What Old Testament stories and characters stand out to you?
• How does understanding the story and message of the Old Testament help us as Christians?

 **Closing**

Praise the Word

Sing or play a song or two derived from the Old Testament. Old favorites include Pharaoh, Pharaoh, Awesome God, El Shaddai, Creation Doo Wah Ditty. Contemporary songs include God of Wonders (Genesis); Better Is One Day (Psalms); Blessed Be Your Name (Job); Forever (Exodus); I Could Sing of Your Love Forever (Creation); Lord Most High (Creation, God of Justice); Over Me (the God of Israel); Give Us Clean Hands (God of Jacob); Here I Am, Lord; Thy Word; Awesome God; Go Down, Moses; We Are Climbing Jacob's Ladder; Great Is Thy Faithfulness.

Bible Challenge

Hold up a Bible. Remind the youth that this book is the story of God, who despite our failings, continues to invite us into a loving relationship and to work with God toward wholeness, justice, and love for all!

Challenge them to 1) read their Bibles this week, 2) to look for Scripture that has special meaning for them, and 3) to bring their Bible with them next week. Sing "Thy Word" to close.

Old Testament Words of Life (Handout on CD)

Give youth a copy of the Old Testament Words of Life Scripture passages. Ask different youth to read a verse. Pause after reading. Close with prayer for the witness of the Word. Encourage students to take the handout home and post it somewhere in their room where they can see it or place it in their Bible.

Out and About

Visit a Jewish synagogue to see how the Scriptures are treated and what role they play in Jewish worship and life. Ask the rabbi to talk about the importance of Torah for the life of Judaism. Tour the synagogue and look for art that represents various stories from the Hebrew Bible.

Service Projects

• Go glean a field. Find out how and why from the Society of St. Andrew. (Link on CD)

• Old Testament Law speaks often of caring for orphans. How can you help orphans today? Think about children left without parents because of AIDS or disasters, such as the Asian tsunami.
(Relief agencies on CD)

Special Events

• Invite a Jewish family to lead the group in the Sabbath ritual and talk about its meaning for them.
• Help the youth learn about the traditions of the Passover Seder Meal, which retells the story of the Exodus with foods and symbolic action.
(Handout on CD)

Youth Witness Statement

• Throughout this series invite various youth to talk about their experience in a Bible study or in reading the Bible.
• Have individual youth quote their favorite Bible passage or tell about their favorite Bible story or person and talk about what the story or person means to them.
(How-to on CD)

Announcements

Be sure to publicize other opportunities for Bible study, such as *3V Bible Studies*, *Synago* groups, *Youth DISCIPLE*, and not-to-be-overlooked Sunday school.(Ordering info on CD)

GOOD NEWS!

Have It Your Way!

Choose from, adapt, or rearrange these elements to create the best soul feast for your youth group.

The Fixin's

More fun stuff to make the theme extra special! Your choice.

Munchies

- Offer some traditional Middle Eastern foods, such as olives, dates, figs, almonds, pistachios, humus, pita bread and dip.
- Praise and reward youth who brought a Bible with them. Give them a "sweet treat, " such as a Kudos® candy bar. Keep encouraging others to bring Bibles for the final week of this Combo.

Worship and Praise Music

- "Holy and Anointed One," featuring Randy Butler (*WOW Worship Orange—Today's 30 Most Powerful Worship Songs*)
- "My Redeemer Lives," by Hillsongs Australia (*Shout to the Lord 2000*)
- "Raise Up the Crown (All Hail the Power of Jesus' Name)," by Passion (*Hymns Ancient and Modern: Live Songs of Our Faith*)
- "O How I Love Jesus"
- "There's Something About That Name"
- "Majesty, Worship His Majesty"
- "Fairest Lord Jesus"
- "Jesus Loves Me"
- "Lord, I Lift Your Name on High"
- "Lord of the Dance"
- "He Lives"
- "In the Garden"
- "I Love to Tell the Story"

SOUL FOOD: Jesus' life, teachings, example, death, and resurrection bring good news and an invitation to follow him!

SCRIPTURE: Philippians 2:1-11 (Every tongue should confess Jesus Christ is Lord.)

Games (Additional game on CD)

Follow Me

Blindfold group members and then lead them around an area using your voice or other sounds. The idea is to have the group members experience what is is like to try to follow someone.

Bible Boggle

Have teams of four to seven persons, each with a Bible, pencil, and paper in hand. Issue the challenge and the instruction to write as many as possible in the time allotted. Set a timer, or call out "Start" and "Stop" after two minutes. Then have someone read his or her list of people in the four Gospels, for example. If anyone else has listed the same person, both players must cross off the entry from their sheet. Only the names that no one else has also listed remain and count as points. Play several rounds with different challenges: places in the Bible, women in the Old or New Testament, books of the Old or New Testament, and so forth.

SHARE AND CARE GROUPS

Checking in: Highs and lows of the week, prayer requests, and prayer

Warm up: Print <u>Jesus Image</u>, and have it ready. Have the group sit in a circle, or multiple circles if you have a large group. (Print a copy of the image for each circle of youth.) Pass the image around the circle and have each person talk about whatever comes to mind as he or she holds the portrait. There are no right or wrong answers. The group members may relate thoughts, feelings, questions, memories—whatever. (<u>Image on CD</u>)

Focus Point

Video Option: Show a scene from Jesus' life from *Jesus of Nazareth or* one of the other movie options. Preview the film and select your scene carefully. Be mindful that certain scenes may be overwhelming. Debrief the group in terms of their reaction to the scene.

Music Option: Sing praise songs about Jesus, then debrief what the songs are saying and what they mean. See the list in the margin on page 76. Most contemporary praise songs focus on Jesus or some aspect of his life. Choose examples that your group loves to sing. This exercise will make those familiar songs more meaningful whenever the group sings them in the future.

Focus Thoughts (Text on CD)

The New Testament continues the story begun in the Old Testament. In the Gospels (*invite the youth to name them*) Jesus enters the story. Jesus is the single most significant person in human history. His teachings and example, and those who follow him, have done more to shape history, culture, art, literature, and our society than any thing else in recorded history. His teachings, life, death, and Resurrection are central to what we as Christians believe and do. Knowing who he was, what he did, and what he taught is crucial to who we are and how we are called to live. Our goal today is to look at the "big picture" of the life and teachings of Jesus.

Let's start with the four Gospels. Why do you think we have four different books about Jesus in our Bible? (*Invite youth responses.*) The writers had different audiences and different emphases. Matthew was writing to show Jews how Jesus was the fulfillment of the Jewish prophesies and hope for a messiah. Mark was writing during a time of persecution; his story was both to encourage Christians and to invite others to follow Jesus, who was the one who ultimately would triumph over evil. Luke focused more on the non-Jewish people, the Gentiles. He lifted up the poor and oppressed.

These three Gospels are called *synoptic,* meaning "one eye." They cover the same basic material, although from different perspectives. John, the fourth Gospel writer, is much less historical and much more spiritual. For John, Jesus is the "Word" that came from God and that is God.

(*Read aloud **John 1:1-5**.*)

In the Gospel of John we move from the Jesus of history to the Christ of faith.

Because of the Christmas season, many of you are already familiar with the stories of Jesus' birth. Today we're jumping ahead to his ministry. Some of you already know parts of Jesus' life. Help me tell the story when you can.

(*Show the PowerPoint® presentation: The Gospels of the New Testament. Intersperse your own comments and additional information to help make this overview come alive for the youth. Let your love for Jesus come through!*)

Now you know his story, but that's not all he wants us to know. Jesus doesn't want to live only in our minds, but in our hearts. This story is about his love for you—so great that he willingly died for your sins. If you have never claimed that love for your life, if you have never said yes to following this living Jesus, now is a good time. Let's pray.

Other Movie Options

Choose one of these other movies, or ask students to recommend a more recent release. Be sure to preview your selection to avoid any content that would be objectionable in your setting. Remember that you must have a video license. (Video licensing information on CD)

• *The Greatest Story Ever Told*
• *Jesus* (Jesus Film Project)

Create-a-Video

Have a volunteer team make a video. They may want to depict one of Jesus' parables, one of his miracles, or an event from his life. One option is to update the event, placing it in their school, their family, or in their church.

On-the-Street Interviews (Questions on CD)

On Screen

Key points in Focus Thoughts (PowerPoint® on CD)

Leader Scripture Exploration

• **Romans 5:12-21** (Christ's act of righteousness leads to justification and life for all.)
• **Ephesians 2:1-10** (From Death to Life)

Out and About

Visit an art museum specifically to look at paintings and artifacts that speak of Jesus. Be sure to talk about the art and the experience.

Service Projects

Follow Jesus' statement of mission from Luke 4:18. (Ideas on CD)

Special Events

• Have your pastor do a service of Holy Communion or a love feast. Point out that the liturgy includes a rehearsal of the biblical story.
• Peter's Walk (Description on CD)

Youth Witness Statement

Have a youth talk about his or her relationship with Christ. Or continue having students talk about their favorite story, verse, or person in the New Testament. (How-to on CD)

Announcements

Be sure to publicize other opportunities for Bible study, such as *3V Bible Studies*, *Synago* groups, *Youth DISCIPLE*, and (not-to-be-overlooked) Sunday school. (Ordering info on CD)

Now What?

Give the youth information about becoming and growing as a Christian. Make available the booklet *Now What? Next Steps for Your New Life in Christ* (Abingdon Press, 2003; ISBN: 068708119X) (Ordering information on CD)

FOCUS GROUP (Additional questions on CD)

• What do you see in the lives of people who are devoted disciples of Jesus that is different from what you see in persons who are not followers?
• Why do you think that Jesus has had such an impact upon people around the world throughout the ages?
• **Read Philippians 2:1-11.** What do you think this statement means: "Let the same mind be in you that was in Christ Jesus"? How would having the same mind as Jesus make a difference in your everyday life?

CLOSING

Praise the Word

Close with a sending forth that builds on the experience of the meeting—discovering Jesus, who loved us so much that he would die for our sin; following Jesus who calls us to love others; sharing Jesus with a hurting world. Here are some suggestions:

• Sing one or two praise songs about Jesus.
• Have the group members write a brief affirmation of what they personally believe about Jesus and have them place it on a cross or at the foot of a cross as an offering.
• Invite the youth to come to the altar to pray. Allow them to leave at their own time.

You may want to observe and then follow up during the week to give individual youth an opportunity to talk about the experience and their commitment. Have on hand copies of *Now What? Next Steps for Your New Life in Christ* to give to youth who are new to the faith.

"At the Name of Jesus" (Litany on CD)

Read this litany based on **Philippians 2:1-11** as a closing. End with singing a song, such as "Lord, I Lift Your Name on High."

Gospel Words of Life (Handout on CD)

THE R ST OF TH STORY— and Me

SOUL FOOD: The story of the first Christians is our story. Their struggles, concerns, and issues are the same as ours. In understanding their faith, we better understand our faith.

SCRIPTURE: Revelation 21:1-5a (God will triumph; the separation between God and humanity will be no more.)

Games

New Testament Wheel of Fortune

If your group liked the Old Testament Wheel of Fortune game, you could do the same thing with the Acts and the letters of the New Testament. You could even reuse the wheel. (Instructions on CD)

New Testament Concentration

Divide the group into two teams. Create the gameboard with cards with hidden words or phrases on the back sides. The cards are on an alphanumeric grid (a, b, c, and so forth down the side; 1, 2, 3, and so forth across). There are two matching cards with each word or phrase. The point of the game is to find the two that are identical. If a team is unsuccessful, the next team tries. The key is to remember where the words are. (Words and phrases on CD)

SHARE AND CARE GROUPS

Checking in: Highs and lows of the week, prayer requests, and prayer

Warm up: In the game, which answers were familiar or easy? Which were new or difficult? What would life be like without the church? (Additional questions on CD)

FOCUS POINT

Video Option: *A.D.* (from *www.christiancinema.com*) tells the story of the book of Acts. Preview the video and select a powerful scene to get your group's attention. An alternative from PBS, is *From Jesus to the Christ: The First Christians*, which is in a documentary format but extremely well done. Be sure to preview your selection. Remember that you must have a video license. (Video licensing information on CD)

Have It Your Way!

Choose from, adapt, or rearrange these elements to create the best soul feast for your youth group.

THE FIXiN'S

More fun stuff to make the theme extra special! Your choice.

Munchies

• Go Italian! Remind the youth that the church spread to Rome. Serve pizza, spaghetti, lasagna, spumoni.
• Praise and reward youth who brought a Bible with them. Give them a "sweet treat, " such as a Kudos® candy bar. Encourage them all to keep their Bible close to them and themselves close to the Word of Life.

Worship and Praise Music

• "God of Wonders," by By the Tree (*Hold You High*)
• "Shout to the Lord," by Matt Redman (*Worship Together: I Could Sing of Your Love Forever*)
• "Holiness"
• "Jesus, Name Above All Names"
• "Lord Most High"
• "You Are So Good to Me," by Third Day (*Offerings II: All I Have to Give*)
• "You Are My All in All," by Natalie Grant (*Worship With Natalie Grant & Friends*)
• "Forever," by Chris Tomlin (*Worship Together: I Could Sing of Your Love Forever*)
• "Give Us Clean Hands," by Chris Tomlin (*Worship Together: Be Glorified*)
• "Great Is Your Love," by Ross King (*Absolute Worship*)
• "Here I Am to Worship," by Tim Hughes (*Here I Am to Worship*)

Create-a-Video

Have a volunteer team make a video. They may want to depict one of the events in Acts. Lively options include: the Pentecost story, conflict between Peter and Paul over whether we must be Jews in order to be Christians, Paul angry with the Galatians and wishing the knife would slip, John and one of the scenes from Revelation.

One option for the youth is to update the event, placing it in their school, their family, or in their church. This approach could be similar to the TV show *Joan of Arcadia*. You might have a Joan or John of your local town, school, or church.

Talk Tip

Be sure that every youth has access to a Bible during the presentation. Encourage them to look for Acts, the various letters, and Revelation.

Background Help

Many Bibles have a page or so of introduction to each book. You may find reading these very helpful as you prepare for this session. Point out these Bible study helps to the youth as well.

 On Screen

Key points in Focus Thoughts (PowerPoint® on CD)

Activity Option: Hand out the "Explosion!" sheet. Invite pairs or threes to work together to make the matches. Post or give the answers after a few minutes, but do not spend time talking about each one. Treat the activity as an appetizer to the story of the church. (Handout on CD)

FOCUS THOUGHTS (Text on CD)

We've been doing this race through the Bible, trying to get the big picture of what this book is all about and why it is so important to us. We've done the B.C. Sprint through the Old Testament and condensed the marathon of Jesus' three-year ministry into just a quick newscast replay! Today we bring the race home. We're looking at what happened after Jesus' resurrection and how that connects with you and me today.

Let's set the context. You remember Jesus had been crucified and risen from the grave; he appeared multiple times to many different people, and then ascended into heaven. Can you imagine the feelings of those who were close to him? Fear, sadness, disappointment, despair, disbelief, joy, confusion, loss! So they gathered, waiting . . . they weren't sure exactly for what. We pick up the story in the Book of Acts.

(*Ask the youth:* What's the full title of the book? That's a clue to the rest of the story.)

Let's think about those apostles. As disciples, they often did not understand what Jesus was telling them; they ran away when Jesus was in trouble; they were generally what we might call "wimps." But at Pentecost God's Spirit came to them in a very dramatic way. It came as wind; it touched the disciples with tongues of fire; it enabled the crowds gathered from all over the known world to hear the message each in their own language! Peter, the one who denied Jesus three times, spoke so boldly to the people about Jesus that day that 5,000 chose to be Christian! The church was born.

Empowered by the Holy Spirit, the apostles and the new converts spread the good news of Jesus Christ. The church grew, and, guess what? The religious authorities got upset! Consequently, persecutions grew also. One early church leader, Stephen, was arrested and stoned to death. Watching was a young Pharisee named Saul, who was leader in the persecutions and who approved the stoning. But that same Saul encountered the spirit of Christ on the road to Damascus and had his life radically changed. He became Paul, the Apostle, and his being on fire for Christ helped spread the Christian faith far beyond Jerusalem.

As Paul and other disciples traveled, new churches came into being. Look at these names of the places where churches were. What do they connect with? (*Names of the letters*)

But for the people in those churches figuring out how to live as a Christian, when Christianity was so new, was difficult. There were lots of controversies. Those folks didn't have the 2,000 years of tradition that we do to help them. But they had Paul! Paul would hear of problems a church was having and write letters to them. After the Book of Acts are twenty-one letters, 14 of them attributed to Paul and 7 to various other apostles. Individually, they deal with various topics.

But together the letters lay out key understandings about Christ and faith; they help develop the way we think about God, that is, our theology. The letters also deal with the practical questions of life in the Spirit and life as a community of faith. As were the Chosen People in the Old Testament, the church is set apart to be a witness to God's love. Our lives, individually and as a community, are to reflect the grace that we have experienced through Christ. We are blessed to be a blessing.

The final book of the Bible is one that many people have questions about. Revelation is filled with amazing and puzzling images that some people have taken out of context to predict the end of the world, for example. Revelation was written during a time of extreme persecution, so the writing is filled with symbols, like a code. But its message was and is to encourage those who are suffering to hang on—God will ultimately triumph!

(*Read aloud **Revelation 21:1-5a**.*)

Revelation is a great book of hope for all Christians.

From this quick look at the last 23 books of the New Testament, three things are especially important for us to keep in mind:

1) The Bible shows us how the Holy Spirit can give people power to live boldly for Christ, even to withstand persecution.
2) The Bible shows us how to live faithfully, in ways that reflect who God is, in ways that bless others. We do that both individually and as a community of faith—the church. We can do that because the Holy Spirit empowers us too!
3) The Bible shows us that God is ultimately in charge; the suffering and evil that are part of this world will be replaced by the kingdom of God. We can live with confidence and joy because we have that hope and assurance. Let's pray.

 **FOCUS GROUP** (Additional questions on CD)

Working together, come up with two to five statements that describe what the Bible is, what it says, and what it means for people today. What would you tell someone who either did not know much about the Bible or who thought the Bible was just a "stuffy old book"?

CLOSING (Additional closing on CD)

Praise the Word

Close by singing one or two praise songs about that reference some of the issues the early church dealt with. You might find the following particularly appropriate: Salvation Spring Up From the Ground, Forever, Give Us Clean Hands, Great Is Your Love, Here I am to Worship.

Bible Challenge

Hold up a Bible. Challenge the youth to go deeper into the Word of God. Include an invitation to Bible study, Bible reading as a devotional practice, memorizing key verses. If you are able, consider giving everyone a new Bible. (Information on CD)

Out and About

Gather at someone's home to watch an episode (live or taped) from *Joan of Arcadia*. If your group is large, split and go to different homes for the session.
(Discussion suggestions on CD)

Service Projects

- Find out what your particular church is doing to serve others. How can the youth be involved?
- Also find out what churches are doing in the world because they have joined together to create greater resources. How can youth contribute? What about a fundraiser? Make those efforts go further by educating the congregation about what the funds are accomplishing through the church's efforts. (Example on CD)

Special Events

- Catacomb Worship
- Romans and Christians
(Descriptions on CD)

Youth Witness Statement

Invite various youth to talk about their experience in a Bible study or in reading the Bible. Or have individual youth quote their favorite Bible passage or tell about their favorite Bible story or person and tell why it is their favorite.

Announcements

Be sure to publicize other opportunities for Bible study, such as *3V Bible Studies*, *Synago* groups, *Youth DISCIPLE*, and not-to-be-overlooked Sunday school!
(Ordering info on CD)

HOUSE OF FAITH

COME ON IN!

From hangin' out on the front porch, to coming inside to live, to going out from the shed, the journey of the Christian faith can be compared to the layout of a house. Persons move through the house as they grow deeper in their relationship with God. These programs encourage the youth to discover God's activity in drawing them closer and providing them a safe home.

APPETIZERS

Publicity Ideas: *Don't neglect advertising (within your church and elsewhere). Use your imagination. Create a timeline for maximum effect. Spread the word with passion.*

- Create a flyer using the <u>theme logo</u> from the CD; include dates, times, and location. Advertise in your church bulletin, in your youth newsletter, and on posters around the church. Send an email blast to your youth; include the logo. (<u>Logo design on CD</u>)

- Find someone to make an announcement posing as a high energy host of a home-renovation television show. Have some assistants with tool boxes or tool belts carry a sign painted on a large piece of plywood or cardboard to communicate the theme and dates.

- Have a young person dressed as a grandmother (or grandfather) make an announcement while seated in a rocking chair. This announcement should sound especially like a down-home, front-porch invitation for the youth. Add your group's own touch to make it as funny as possible.

COMBOS MENU

Main Dishes

Weekly Program Options: *Choose one or all; do in any order. Check each description for the fixin's.*

1. **Hangin' Out on the Front Porch**—We all want to be invited and included, but sometimes we shy away from God's invitation to "sit awhile." God continues to invite us into relationship.

2. **The Living Room**—Where is that place where everyone gathers, the place where everyone relaxes and shares life? Growing as a Christian is best within the context of community, a group of fellow travelers. The church is our "living room."

3. **Out of the Shed**—Anyone can accumulate a collection of tools, but Christians are called to put them to use. As a Christian grows in faith, there also comes a desire to respond by serving. God gives us tools to serve others.

4. **Safe at Home**—We live in a world that is not safe nor free from conflict, but as Christians we have peace—not as the world defines, but as Jesus gives.

SPICE IT UP

Theme Decorations: *Look at your space. Use your imagination. Give away or auction off decorations as prizes at the end of the theme.*

- Build a scaled-down house. Using plywood or other building materials construct an A-frame house slightly larger than a doll house. Include some kind of a front porch, living room, and shed or garage. Or find a child's plastic playhouse (like you might find in a backyard or church playground) and ask to borrow it for the duration of the theme.

- Add to or emphasize the "hominess" of your meeting space. Add throw pillows, blankets, and soft lighting. Consider compiling collections of pictures from your group's outings and adventures and hang them on the walls as you might find in the home of a proud parent or grandparent.

- Add rocking chairs and other types of "front-porch" furniture.

- Download the sign for "Safe Place." Make copies and post them. <u>(Link on CD)</u>

DRINKS

" 'Lord, when was it that we saw you . . . thirsty and gave you something to drink? . . . ' 'Truly, I tell you, just as you did it to one of the least of these' " (Matthew 25:37, 40a).

Service project ideas

Hangin' Out on the Front Porch

Have It Your Way!

Choose from, adapt, or rearrange these elements to create the best soul feast for your youth group.

The Fixin's

More fun stuff to make the theme extra special! Your choice.

Munchies

- Have the youth make Graham Cracker Houses. These fun houses are easily constructed using graham crackers and cement icing. You simply cement crackers together with frosting. When they're dry, let the youth decorate them with their favorite candies. The builders can munch on the building supplies! (Instructions on CD)
- Old Fashioned Lemonade
- Tropical Lemonade
- Front Porch Gingersnaps

Popular Songs

Use these before and/or after the program to engage the youth. These are some options. Try to include the latest appropriate popular songs.

- "Stay," by 12 Stones (*Potter's Field*)
- "You've Got a Friend," by James Taylor (*James Taylor: Greatest Hits*)
- "Home," by Rich Mullins (*Songs 2*)

Worship and Praise Music

- "Lemonade Song," Mitch McVicker (*Mitch McVicker*)
- "Prepare the Way," by Passion (*Our Love Is Loud*)
- "Big House," by Audio Adrenaline (*Don't Censor Me*)

SOUL FOOD: Whether we know it or not, God has invited each of us to develop a deeper relationship. Every day is an opportunity to respond.

SCRIPTURE: John 5:2-17 (Jesus healed the lame man, who then reported it to the Jews.)

Games (Additional game on CD)

Renovation Race

Prepare equal piles of building blocks such as interlocking children's toys. Divide the youth into equal teams, with teams lined up across from a pile. On your instruction a member from each team will race to the designated pile and bring back a piece for the team to use to build a house. When each team has used all of their pieces, ask youth or volunteers to vote on the house that looks most like a house, the most creative, the sturdiest construction.

Lemonade Taste-Test

Prepare a variety of lemonade and lemon-flavored drink mixes. Pour the drinks into nondescript cups enough for several taste-test stations. Using the labels or containers, challenge the youth to determine which drink is which brand. Is it sugar free? instant? fresh squeezed? The team with the most correct guesses is treated to a full pitcher of their favorite taste-test drink.

Share and Care Groups (Text on CD)

Checking in: Highs and lows of the week, prayer requests, and prayer

Warm up: Where is the place that you feel most comfortable? What are the best places to get to know another person or group of people: during class? at games? at restaurants? Have you ever passed up an invitation to a party or get-together? Why? Have you ever ignored or passed up an invitation from God?

Focus Point

Video Options: *The Truman Show* (1998) (Start: 1:29; stop: 1:36) Truman leaves his perfect, but phony, world to explore real life to see what he's missing. The phony "creator" tries to convince Truman to stay. (Note: The phony creator says a two-word expletive during this scene.)

Activity Option: Welcome Mats—Discuss ways to make youth group and church more welcoming. Then have the youth design a welcome mat for your meeting space. Ask, "What kinds of feelings or images would a stranger have when he or she saw this mat?" Have the group or individuals use paper and paints to construct a welcome mat. (Note: You may start with a basic mat from a home-furnishing store, if you'd like.)

Focus Thoughts (Text on CD)

Sometimes it seems easier to just ignore a call or an invitation than to respond. Once when I was working in an office, I discovered that I didn't know how to correctly forward a phone call to the correct person. I tried several times, but each time the call ended up being disconnected. I'm pretty sure that I knew what I was doing, I pushed the "transfer" button then the extension of the person the call was for. It's worked in every other office I've spent time in. It was probably a problem with the phone—surely.

Anyway, there came a point when I no longer wanted to answer the phone. So I ignored it when it rang. There were plenty of other people who were perfectly capable of answering the phone and transferring the call to the correct person. You know what I discovered? The fact that I wasn't answering the phone did not stop the phone from ringing. People still called and usually someone answered—just not me!

God continues to call us, kind of like a ringing phone. God continues to invite us to spend time getting to know God. Did you know that there's nothing that God wants more than for you to learn about and experience a relationship with God through Jesus Christ?

Does the house or apartment you live in have a front porch? It's not as common anymore, but front porches or steps used to be gathering places in neighborhoods. Front porches usually had chairs or swings and other furnishings to encourage visiting. It was not unusual to be invited for conversation and a glass of lemonade by neighbors as you walked by their house. The front porch was a great place to hang out.

In the Scripture is a story of a man who spent years on the porch (called a portico) near a pool. Let's hear his story.

(*Read aloud* **John 5:2-17.**)

What was Jesus' invitation to the lame man? He invited him to "Stand up, take up your mat, and walk." The Jewish people gathered there were upset that Jesus had healed on the Sabbath. When they questioned him, Jesus did not deny that he had done this and proclaimed, "My father is still working, and I also am working." The invitation to be healed through faith in God is still very much extended to us today. God is still working; God continues to invite us. I guess you could say that God does things the old-fashioned way. You're still invited to spend time on the front porch with God.

Return now, in your mind, to the front porch in the neighborhood image. After some time spent on the porch, you and your neighbor may eventually decide to take the conversation inside. Maybe it has become a little too cold outside; maybe you'll share a meal together, or look at photo albums of family adventures and accomplishments. When you come inside, you know that you have crossed the threshold into a deeper relationship.

Other Movie Options

Choose one of these movies, or ask students to recommend a more recent release. Be sure to preview your selection to avoid any content that would be objectionable in your setting. Remember that you must have a video license.
(Video licensing information on CD)

• *Running Scared* (1986) (R)
• *The Muppet Movie* (1979)
• *The Fugitive* (1993)

Leader Scripture Exploration

• **Isaiah 12** (Praise God for comfort)
• **Luke 2:41-52** (Jesus in his Father's house)

On Screen

Key points from Focus Thoughts (PowerPoint® and Text on CD)

Create-a-Video

Invite a team in advance to retell the story of the healing of the lame man and the controversy that followed. They can stay with the biblical story and setting or change to a contemporary situation or setting. Videotape the drama and show it.

Out and About

If your church is in a community setting, gather on the front steps or entryway of the building. If your church is not in a high-traffic area, you might ask the owner of a nearby shop if you can borrow his or her front stoop, or consider a park or town square. Once assembled, offer lemonade and conversation to passersby.

If needed, supply the youth with ice-breaker questions to assist with their conversations (for example, ask about their favorite kind of lemonade, and then tell about the taste-test game.) Encourage the youth to tell the passersby what group they are with and why they are offering lemonade. You might be surprised at the number of people who are willing to spend a few minutes chatting.

Service Projects

- Take the candy houses to children who are ill or to older adults who need cheering up! Deliver them and make the visit the ministry.
- Build a ramp or make improvements to the front steps of the home of a church or community member.

(Additional idea on CD)

Witness Statement

Invite a youth or an adult to tell about his or her experience of recognizing that God is "still working."
(How-to on CD)

God also wants to bring you into a deeper relationship. Once you've visited on the front porch, God will open a new door, inviting you to invest yourself in a journey toward commitment and discipleship. But the decision to go inside that door, to make a commitment to developing a deeper relationship with God, has to be made by you. The invitation is there; the door is open, but only you can take that step.

Are you hanging out on the front porch, perhaps just coming to youth group because your friends are here? Jesus invites you to pick yourself up and come inside, to become whole, like the lame man. He decided to trust Jesus, and he was healed!

Many of you have already made that choice, but there are people you know who have not. Or maybe you've been on the front porch for years; it's time now to risk walking into the house. It's time to risk answering the call of God—even if you're not sure that you know how to work the phones. You're invited to stand up, take up your mat, and walk through the door! Let's pray.

Focus Group (Questions on CD)

- Where do you see yourself in the story of the lame man and those who questioned Jesus' authority?
- What kinds of questions would you ask God if you were sipping a glass of lemonade on God's front porch? (*Record responses to this question and bring them to the closing.*)
- What can we do to help our friends who don't know about God's invitation to be welcomed and get to know God?

Closing

Accepting the Invitation

Provide time at the altar. Remind the youth that God welcomes them on the front porch, but that the door to a deeper relationship is open for them. Pray too for commitments to invite others to youth group, as a "front-porch" of faith.

Sippin' and Listenin'

Have the youth join you in the most relaxed area of your meeting space. This may simply be the floor. Ask the youth to ask the questions they recorded in their Focus Group. Select questions to be used in a closing prayer. Ask volunteers to read the questions again during the prayer and wait for 20–30 seconds before the next one is read to allow time to hear from God. After the prayer, take the questions and lay them on the front porch of the house you are using as a theme piece.

The Lord Is My Friend

Close with this paraphrase of Psalm 23. Encourage the youth to take the handout home and put it where they will see it from time to time as a reminder of the One who wants to be their friend. (Handout on CD)

THE LIVING ROOM

SOUL FOOD: As Christians on earth, we are never "done." God wants us to always learn more about God's ways and to grow together as God's people. This is why we have one another; this is why we have the church.

SCRIPTURE: Acts 2:42-47 (The early Christians devoted themselves to learning and fellowship—"doing life" together as the church.)

GAMES (Additional game on CD)

Room Builders

Divide the youth into groups of 5–6. Give the teams three minutes to build a living room, using only their bodies. The youth must use their imagination to form couches, lamps, magazine racks, ceiling fans, and so on. Every team member must be a part of the living room for a team to win.

Room-Size Tic-Tac-Toe

Set up nine chairs in three rows of three to create a life-size tic-tac-toe playing field. Divide the youth into two groups. Have each team send one player at a time to fill in a chair. The first team to get three in a row wins the round. Keep playing until you have a clear winner. If your group is large, set up more than one tic-tac-toe grid of chairs and additional teams. Include the adult visitors in the teams.

SHARE AND CARE GROUPS (Text on CD)

Checking in: Highs and lows of the week, prayer requests, and prayer

Warm up: Name something you like to do by yourself. Name something that you couldn't do on our own. Why are some things easier to accomplish with help from others? Name one person who has helped you to know God better. What did that person do?

FOCUS Point

Video Option: *Stand by Me* (Scene 17 "Gordie Dreams"). Gordie's brother died; Chris demonstrates his caring as he listens. Other scenes are also strong (#13 & #18) but have language that is problematic. Be sure to preview your selection to avoid any content that would be objectionable in your setting. Remember you must have a video license. (Licensing information on CD)

Have It Your Way!

Choose from, adapt, or rearrange these elements to create the best soul feast for your youth group.

THE FIXIN'S

More fun stuff to make the theme extra special! Your choice.

Munchies

- Couch Potatoes (Baked potatoes with the works)
- Bowls of popcorn (living room fare)

Add Church Members

Invite additional adults of all ages, including parents, to be part of this session. Have them simply be there and participate with the youth. You may want to ask a few to tell their story of how the church as been important to them (see Panel Option of Focus Point, On-the-Street Interviews, and Witness Statement). For congregation members—youth and adults—to know one another is an important element in being the church.

Popular Songs

Use these before and/or after the program to engage the youth. These are some options. Try to include the latest appropriate popular songs.

- "Homeless," by Paul Simon (*Graceland*)
- "Sometimes You Can't Make It on Your Own," by U2 (*How to Dismantle an Atomic Bomb*)

Worship and Praise Music

- "Church," by Derek Webb (*She Must and Shall Go Free*)
- "Big House," Audio Adrenaline (*Don't Censor Me*)
- "On Christ the Solid Rock"
- "We Are the Church"
- "Blest Be the Tie That Binds"
- "How Beautiful," Twila Paris (*Cry for the Desert*)

On-the-Street Interviews

Ask church members why the church is important to them. Videotape the interviews.

Leader Scripture Exploration

- **Psalm 133** (Unity is precious and blessed by God.)
- **1 Corinthians 12:12-31** (We are the body of Christ designed to function together.)

 **On Screen**

Key Points from Focus Thoughts (PowerPoint® and Text on CD)

Panel Option: Ask three or four individuals (youth and adults) to talk about why the church is important to them. Invite the audience to follow up with questions to the panel.

FOCUS THOUGHTS (Text on CD)

One of my favorite things to do is to go backpacking in the mountains. I always go with at least one friend; but at certain points in each trip, I like to head off on my own to think and to pray and mostly be alone. I really enjoy having time to be by myself.

But do you know the first thing I do when I return from one of these trips? I find someone who will care enough to listen, and I describe in great detail what I experienced. I want to tell someone about it. I want to share with someone else what I originally enjoyed doing alone.

It's difficult to keep something to yourself when you're excited about it. I think maybe that's a part of the reason the church started off the way it did. Listen to these verses that describe the early church:

(*Read aloud Acts 2:41-47.*)

The first Christians were so excited about the gospel—the good news that Jesus opened the door to a relationship with God—that they changed their day-to-day lives and devoted themselves to that relationship. They were eager for the disciples to teach them. They wanted to be with other Christians. They ate meals together—not just on Sunday after church or occasionally on Wednesday nights, but they ate together in one another's homes regularly. They celebrated Holy Communion, and they prayed together. They helped one another follow God more faithfully. They spent all of this time together because they experienced in the Christian community the deep love that is a gift of God. They gained "glad and generous hearts." They grew in faith and also in numbers.

In our homes, many of us have living rooms or another room in the house where people tend to gather. Maybe it's the kitchen or den or dining room. In our gathering places, we talk about our day at school or work. We vent our frustrations. We enjoy simply being together; we may even pray together. Here we share our lives with people we love and who love us.

Maybe you've never thought about it quite this way, but the church is kind of like that too. It's our "living room," the place where we share our lives together. You know that the church is not just the building—rather, it's the people of God gathered. Among these people—in this "living room"—we share a living faith.

That's why we're here. That's why it's important that you keep coming to church—even on days when you don't really feel all that close to God. God and God's people will meet you here so that you too will know the good news of the gospel and live with a glad and generous heart. Let's pray.

 **F⊙CUS GR⊙UP** (Questions on CD)

- What do you like about church?
- What do you get here that you don't get in other places?
- Who in the church has listened to you or helped you have a stronger faith in God? (*Record responses to this question on note cards and bring them to the closing.*)

 **CL⊙SING**

Honoring God's Church

Have the youth join you in the most relaxed area of your meeting space, which may simply be the floor. Invite the youth to tell about a person in the church who has influenced their faith. Ask them to place their responses during the closing prayer in the living room of the house you are using as a center-piece for this theme.

We Are Christians

Explain that symbols have been used throughout time by Christians to help identify one another in the world. When Christians were being persecuted by the Roman Empire, the sign of the fish became a "code" to communicate a Christian's identity in an undercover way.

Hand out a small fish-shaped object. (Christian bookstores sell these as key chains, pins, and so forth.) Encourage your youth to be constantly reminded of their identity as Christians who are seeking to grow in their faith.

Service Projects

- Visit church members who are confined to their homes or a nursing home. Ask them about their faith. Prepare a special gift and/or group prayer that may serve as encouragement and as a reminder that they remain connected to the church.

- Distribute door hangers, inviting people to your church. (Information on CD)

Out and About

- Take a tour of selected areas in your church. For example, does your church have a history room? Visit it. look at old photos, talk about being part of the "great cloud of witnesses" and the ministries of the church in the past. Does your church have a parlor or "living room"? Have your message there. Talk about the church as place we are invited to be comfortable because we are known and loved.

- Visit a church-related ministry that visibly provides a helping hand and encouragement to others. If it is after hours, meet in the empty facility, talk about the ministry that takes place there and say a blessing for the ministry site.

Youth Witness Statement

Invite a youth or an adult church member to talk about how he or she came to the church and why? Have the person talk about what is important to him or her about being part of the church.

OUT OF THE SHED

Have It Your Way!
Choose from, adapt, or rearrange these elements to create the best soul feast for your youth group.

The Fixin's
More fun stuff to make the theme extra special! Your choice.

Munchies

• Make Sawdust Cupcakes by sprinkling standard frosted cupcakes with toasted shredded coconut.

• Instead of a snack this week, have your group use cooking tools to prepare food for persons in your church who are unable to leave home.

Popular Songs

Use these before and/or after the program to engage the youth. These are some options. Try to include the latest appropriate popular songs.

• "Yahweh," by U2 (*How to Dismantle an Atomic Bomb*)
• "Change the World," by P.O.D. (*Payable on Death*)
• "Share the Well," by Caedmon's Call (*Share the Well*)

Worship and Praise Music

• "Take My Life, and Let It Be Consecrated"
• "Every Move I Make," by David Crowder (*The Lime CD*)
• "Offering," by Third Day (*Offerings II: All I Have to Give*)
• "Jesu, Jesu"

SOUL FOOD:
When we allow ourselves to be made stronger in faith, God uses us to further the work of Christ through our service to others.

SCRIPTURE:
1 Corinthians 3:5-9 (We are God's fellow workers.)

Games

Horse and Carriage

Set up a course in a large room with hard flooring. Break into groups of 3–4. One person sits on a large unfolded blanket while the other team members pull them through the course. The first team to cross the line or the team with the best time wins.

Wheelbarrow Tapehead

Divide the youth into pairs. Have pairs line up along a straight line across from a line of various objects (1 of each item per pair): dime, slip of paper, inflated balloon, paper clip, and any other items that you find will work (test to make sure). One partner places a ring of ordinary transparent or masking tape (sticky side out) around a bandanna or hat on his or her head. That team member is "the wheelbarrow." The wheelbarrow's partner is "the farmer." The farmer holds onto and supports the wheelbarrow's ankles and steers the wheelbarrow to and from the items. All pairs will race simultaneously to pick up the objects at the other line, using only the tapehead on the wheelbarrow. Then the items must be returned to the starting line. The pair that returns with the most items in 3 minutes is the winning pair.

⊙ Share and Care Groups

Checking in: Highs and lows of the week, prayer requests, and prayer

⊙ **Warm up:** If possible, bring a tool to show the youth. Tell them about it—what it does, how often you use it, where you can get it, and so forth Ask: What tool do you use best? Do you think that God uses tools? Explain. If you could be a tool, what would you choose? Why? (Questions on CD)

Focus Point

Video Options: *Life Is Beautiful* (Scenes 18–20) Sent to a concentration camp, the father weaves an elaborate story of a game to keep his young son safe. Ultimately, the father sacrifices himself to save the child.

Mission Trip Review/Preview Option: If your youth have been on a mission trip in the past, show the photographs and tell about it. If your youth have not gone, perhaps a group from another church could do a presentation. Be sure to invite the youth to talk about both what they did for others and what the experience did for them.

If you are planning a mission trip or local service project, have the youth do a "commercial" for the upcoming trip or project. You may want the volunteers to create the skit and videotape it so that you can use it other times too to promote participation.

Focus Thoughts (Text on CD)

(*Use a tool-story that comes from your own experience.*) I have an electric sander in my garage. It was a present that I received several years ago. I was very excited to get it. It's small; it fits in the palm of the hand. But I couldn't even tell you whether it works or not. I've never tried it.

It's probably not a big deal. The sander cost only $20 or so. But the thing that worries me is that if I don't work, I might be like that sander. I was purchased by God (for quite a bit more than $20—the price was God's Son Jesus). I was invited into a relationship with God; and I have grown in my faith, thanks to the work of the Holy Spirit through the church. If God has done all of this, and I still "sit on the shelf," then I'm not a very good tool. I've got to get out of the shed and get to work!

What kind of a tool are you? God has invited you to move past just hangin' out on the front porch, to come into the "living room" and experience God's gift of love and acceptance. Like the early Christians, you are growing in faith each time you choose to be with God's people in the church—learning, being in fellowship, partaking of Holy Communion, and praying together. But the "front porch" and the "living room" aren't the only way to think of a house of faith. There's also the "shed" filled with tools waiting to be used for God's good work.

The church at Corinth in the Bible was having some problems with jealousy. They had been learning about Jesus from two different men, Apollos and Paul. Some folks in the church lost sight of whose followers they were called to be. Instead of focusing on Jesus, some began to claim loyalty to Apollos—and others to Paul. Paul wrote to them to set them straight.

(*Read aloud **1 Corinthians 3:5-9**.*)

The Scriptures tell us that God gives us unique gifts to serve. And when we use our gifts, we are effective tools for God. Some of you are gifted at planting seeds. People see and hear that you are different. They want to know what it is that makes you different, and you share your faith. You plant seeds. Others of you are gifted at watering. You take care of people. You offer help; you love them and encourage them as they grow. You are a good friend.

Like Paul and Apollos, we are called to put our special gifts, our unique tools to work. God constantly invites us to discover a deeper faith. God created the church to help us grow stronger. When we work together to serve others, it is God who is working through us for our common purpose. We can trust God to give the growth! Let's pray.

Other Movie Options

Choose this movie, or ask students to recommend a more recent release. Be sure to preview your selection to avoid any content that would be objectionable in your setting. Remember that you must have a video license.
(Video licensing information on CD)

• *Vertical Limit* (2000)
• *Pay It Forward* (2000)
• *The Messenger: The Story of Joan of Arc* (1999)
• *Driving Miss Daisy* (1990)

Leader Scripture Exploration

• **Matthew 20:28** (Jesus came to serve.)
• **Mark 1:31** (The desire to serve after God has touched our lives)

On Screen

Key points from Focus Thoughts (PowerPoint® and Text on CD)

Guest Speaker

Invite a missionary to come tell about serving God in the mission field. Ask about the tools used, and the ways that he or she feels that God has used him or her as a tool.

Out and About

Meet in a workshop. Find a member of the church or community who would be willing to open up his or her garage or shop to your group. Ask your host to describe the work he or she does in the space and tools used.

 Service Projects

• Identify an older member of your church who could use some assistance with garden or yard work. Send one or two persons in advance to talk with the homeowner to find out what needs to be done and what tools (lawn mower, for example) would be available on site. On the work day, assign crews to various areas. Take time to instruct persons about safety and effective use of the tools. Also, be sure to identify what's *not* a weed! Plant some blooming annuals to add some color and delight in the garden.

Have crews take a break at different times and visit with the homeowner, inviting him or her to tell stories about the garden, about being part of the church, about ways he or she has been in service to others through the years. Bring refreshments!

• Team up with some knowledgeable builders and repair persons to provide home repair for community members who are in need. Make sure to involve the youth in the planning and in gathering tools, as well in the work.

(Additional ideas on CD)

Witness Statement

Invite a youth or an adult to talk about his or her experience in serving others. (How-to on CD)

 FOCUS GROUP (Questions on CD)

• What gifts has God given you?
• Have you ever allowed yourself to be used as a tool for God? Describe.
• In what ways is God calling you to use your gifts?
• How could the youth at your church be in service to others? (*Record responses to this question on note cards and bring them to the closing.*)

CLOSING

Seeking to Serve

Have the youth join you in the most relaxed area of your meeting space, which may simply be the floor. Ask the youth to share their ideas for being in service. Have them attach their responses to the door of the shed or garage (if it's large enough) or place them inside the house you are using as a center-piece. Close with the prayer below or one of your own.

Continue, Please, God (Handout on CD)

ONE: Holy God, we are aware that you walk with us along each step in our faith journey.

ALL: You are steady and sure, while we are oftentimes less confident in our faith.

ONE: For those of us lingering on the fringes of the front porch of faith ...

ALL: Continue to call us, continue to invite us.

ONE: For those of us who are taking the steps to know you more intimately ...

ALL: Continue to guide us, continue to shape us.

ONE: For all of us who desire to respond to the gift of faith by serving others ...

ALL: Continue to encourage us, continue to use us.

ONE: Thank you, God, for calling us yours ...

ALL: And for calling us home. Amen.

Safe at Home

SOUL FOOD: God wants us to experience peace in our lives. It's possible to know that peace through Jesus Christ.

SCRIPTURE: John 14:27 (Jesus promises peace to his followers.)

Games (Additional game on CD)

Tag

Play a classic game of tag. Designate a "home base," where runners are safe for as long as they are there.

My Piece I Leave With You

Locate at least three children's jigsaw puzzles with only a few total pieces. Number the back of each piece so that all of the pieces from a given puzzle have the same number, or make the game more challenging and don't number them. Mix the pieces together and hand them out to the youth. Without talking, the youth must assemble the puzzles in a set amount of time.

Share and Care Groups (Text on CD)

Checking in: Highs and lows of the week, prayer requests, and prayer

Warm up: Many communities have designated "Safe Places" where young people know they can go and find protection. Often times these places are stores, churches, hospitals, or police stations. Does your community have such places? Where are they? What are some reasons young people might choose to go to a "Safe Place"? Where do you feel most safe? How is this group a safe place for you emotionally? What can we do to ensure that everyone feels safe here?

Focus Point

Video Option: *Home Alone* (Scene 9 "I'm the Man of the House") Kevin's feeling pretty smug until he encounters the dreaded Mr. Marley; Kevin instinctively rushes home for safety.

Skit Option: Arrange for one or two youth or adult volunteers to prepare a skit involving a baseball player and a home plate umpire. An actual base pad and umpire's mask will add to the skit but are not necessary. (Script on CD)

Have It Your Way!

Choose from, adapt, or rearrange these elements to create the best soul feast for your youth group.

The Fixin's

More fun stuff to make the theme extra special! Your choice.

Munchies

- Baseball fare, such as sunflower seeds or hot dogs
- Comfort foods, such as macaroni and cheese, mashed potatoes, or hot chocolate

Popular Songs

Use these before and/or after the program to engage the youth. These are some options. Try to include the latest appropriate popular songs.

- "Not Coming Home," by Maroon 5 (*Songs About Jane*)
- "All the Way Home," by Andrew Peterson (*Carried Along*)
- "The Long Way Home," by Norah Jones (*Feels Like Home*)

Worship and Praise Music

- "Sometimes by Step," by Rich Mullins (*Songs*)
- "Peace," by Rich Mullins (*Songs 2*)
- "Big House," by Audio Adrenaline (*Don't Censor Me*)
- "That Where I Am, There You …," by Rich Mullins (*Jesus Record*)
- "Because He Lives"
- "Go Now in Peace"

 ## Other Movie Options

Choose one of these movies, or ask students to recommend a more recent release. Be sure to preview your selection to avoid any content that would be objectionable in your setting. Remember that you must have a video license.
(Video licensing information on CD)

- *The Natural* (1984)
- *The Sandlot* (1993)
- *Cold Mountain* (2003) (R)
- *The Terminal* (2004)

Leader Exploration Scriptures

- **Isaiah 9:2-7** (The Prince of Peace)
- **Philippians 4:4-7** (The peace of God will guard your heart and mind in Christ.)
- **1 John 5:9-13** (Peace in the knowledge of salvation)

On Screen

Key Points from Focus Thoughts (PowerPoint® and Text on CD)

Guest Speaker

Invite as a speaker a community member associated with a designated "Safe Place" or other organization that functions as a haven for troubled people. Ask questions about his or her role in providing this service or ministry to community. What challenges do young people face that cause them to enter the door of their "safe place"?
(Link to Safe Place Services on CD)

FOCUS THOUGHTS (Text on CD)

Home is not always a safe place for everyone. For many young people, and maybe for some of you, home is not the safest place for a number of reasons. Unfortunately, abuse and neglect can be in what appear to be the very best of homes. Even the most loving homes are not perfect.

People often equate safety with peace. We think that in order to have peace, we must have safety. Most of us spend our lives trying to feel secure, financially, physically, and even spiritually. We protect our homes and cars and possessions with alarms. We do all of these things in hopes of experiencing peace.

People often equate the absence of conflict with peace. If no one is upset, angry, or fighting, then we have peace. At Christmas, we sing about peace on earth; but the rest of the year (and even at Christmas), we see the news of this war or that attack—often done in the name of bringing peace.

Jesus says that real peace will come from him. In our Scripture today, Jesus is talking to his disciples. These were his closest followers; they had left everything to be with him—no hangin' out on the front porch to see how things would go! They just jumped right in to the living room, spending every day with Jesus, listening as he taught, watching him heal people physically and spiritually.

In the chapter before today's verse, Jesus had just washed their feet, telling them through his own actions to get out of the shed and put their gifts to work in serving others. Let's listen to Jesus' promise to his disciples:

(*Read aloud **John 14:27**.*)

This conversation took place not long before Jesus was crucified. Jesus knew what was coming; they did not. Jesus knew that people were beginning to look to him as the long-expected Messiah, the one who would bring peace, which meant to them getting rid of the Romans—a military overthrow! But Jesus said that his peace was not "as the world gives." It's not the same as the absence of conflict; it's not the same as security.

Jesus knew that he would face beatings and death, that the disciples would face loss and fear—big time. But he said, "Do not let your hearts be troubled, and do not let them be afraid." What *was* he thinking?

Jesus also knew that death would not be final. Resurrection would come. He wasn't simply saying to the disciples, "Don't worry." He wasn't saying that the world would magically change.

Rather, he was promising that in the face of their disappointment, grief, and fear, they would not be abandoned—because Resurrection was coming!

As Christians, we still live in a world of hurt. Not all people are safe—even in their own homes. Conflict swirls around us in greater and lesser degrees from war to misunderstandings and arguments. Our lives are not always peaceful, but as Christians we have the peace of Christ. We have the good news that we are not alone, that God will help us find the strength to face whatever life brings. We live with hope despite our troubles because we know that the Resurrection came. That sure knowledge is the source of the very real peace that Jesus offers us. Let's pray.

 # FOCUS GROUP

- When have you experienced the peace of Christ? (*Record responses to this question on note cards and bring them to the closing.*)
- If you've experienced it, how can you share the peace of Christ with others?

 # CLOSING

Claiming the Peace of Christ

Have the youth join you in the most relaxed area of your meeting space, which may simply be the floor. Invite the youth to share their recorded answers from the Focus Group. Ask them to place their responses in the doorway of the house you are using as a center piece for the theme.

Play "Peace," by Rich Mullins, as a time of meditation or sing the hymn "Because He Lives." You may also wish to have the group to affirm their faith, reading the statement of faith below, or close with a prayer or by reading the Scripture again.

 ## A Statement of Faith (Handout on CD)

Peace I Leave With You

Close by repeating this verse (**John 14:27**). Encourage the youth to memorize it. Give them the poster to take home as a reminder.

Out and About

- Hold your meeting on a baseball field. Incorporate the parts of the field into the theme (that is, the dugout is similar to the front porch because one is watching and learning, and so on).

Service Projects

- Create tags that have spaces for address and other important contact information. Give them to parents of children in your church or community to attach to the shoes or jackets of their children. Help them find their way home if they get lost.

- Initiate a Safe Place for your community. (Information on CD)

Posters (Designs on CD)

My peace I give to you. (Two versions)

Youth Witness Statement

Invite a youth to talk about his or her experience of relying on God and finding peace in a difficult situation or circumstance. (How-to on CD)

COMBOS CD-ROM

Starting the Program

PC/Windows®
The CD-Rom is designed to automatically start when you insert it into your PC. If it does not start automatically, you will need to run the Combos application.

Bring up your directory listing (on Microsoft®, use Explore or My Computer). You will see one subdirectory, "combos," and two files, "autorun" and "Combos." Double-click on the Combos application.

Macintosh®
Double-click on the CD-Rom icon. A pop-up window will appear with OS9 or OSX as options. Double-click on the icon that matches your computer's operating system.

If you get an error message that says, "Could not find the application program…," choose your browser application (for example, Internet Explorer, Netscape, Safari). Once you have done this, you should not have the error message upon opening the CD-Rom in the future.

You can access the subdirectory in the folder named "combos" before you choose your operating system or by clicking on an item such as a presentation or a poster.

Handouts, Presentations, Logos, Posters, Talks

Handouts and some of the other files on the CD-Rom are saved in Adobe Acrobat® (pdf files). To open them, you will need the Adobe Acrobat® Reader installed on your computer. If you do not have Adobe Acrobat® Reader, log on to the Internet while running the CD; click on the Adobe Acrobat® Reader link at the bottom of any page. This will take you to the page where you can download the free reader from Adobe.

On a Macintosh: If you click on a pdf link and receive an error message labeled "Unhandled File Type," choose "Application" and then find the Adobe Acrobat® application on your hard drive.

Presentations that say "PowerPoint®" will launch in your PC browser window. If you have Microsoft® PowerPoint® on your computer and wish to save or modify the presentations, you can click Save As and save them to your hard drive. (On a Macintosh, a directory of PowerPoint® presentations will open. The presentation file that you clicked on is highlighted. Double-click the file to open it, or click and hold your mouse and drag the file to your desktop if you want to save or modify the presentation.)

To get editable text from the **Talks** is to highlight the text from the Focus Thoughts version that you want and copy it, then paste it into your word processing program.

If you want to save any of the files—handouts, presentations, logos, posters—to your hard drive, you can also go to the Combos sub-directory (on Microsoft®, use Explore or My Computer). **Posters** and **theme_logos** have their own sub-directory under the Combos sub-directory. PowerPoint® presentations can be found in the sub-directory for the theme. For instance, if you want the PowerPoint® presentation for the Awesome Power of Perseverance, click on the 05_AWESOME sub-directory; then click on the 02_perseverance.ppt file.

Minimum System Requirements

PC/Windows®
Pentium® II 300 MHz or faster processor
Microsoft® Windows 98 or later
64 MB RAM
4X CD-ROM Drive
Internet Explorer 5.0 or Higher Recommended
QuickTime® 5.0 or higher
External speakers recommended

Macintosh®
PowerPC 300 MHZ or faster processor
Mac OS 9.0 or later
64 MB RAM
4X CD-ROM Drive
Internet Explorer 5.0 or Higher Recommended for OS9
Safari or Internet Explorer Recommended for OS X
QuickTime® 5.0 or higher

Abingdon Technical Support

If you have difficulty launching the program, you may call Abingdon technical support at 615-749-6777, Monday through Friday, 8 a.m. to 5 p.m., Central Standard Time.